WINGS OF WAR

LT. STARK, AUTHOR.

WINGS
OF WAR

An Airman's diary
of the last year
of the war

BY

RUDOLF STARK

Translated into English by
CLAUD W. SYKES

CASEMATE
Philadelphia & Oxford

This edition of *Wings of War* is published in
the United States of America and Great Britain in 2015 by
CASEMATE PUBLISHERS
908 Darby Road, Havertown, PA 19083 and
10 Hythe Bridge Street, Oxford, OX1 2EW

 *A Greenhill Book*

ISBN 978-1-61200-187-6
Digital Edition: ISBN 978-1-61200-188-3

Cataloging-in-publication data is available from the Library of Congress
and the British Library.

PUBLISHING HISTORY:
Wings of War by Rudolf Stark was first published as *Die Jagdstaffel unsere Heimat—
Ein Flieger-Tagebuch aus dem letzten Kriegsjahr,* in Leipzig, Germany by K. F. Koehler
Verlag in 1932. It was first published in the UK (translated by Claude W. Sykes)
by John Hamilton Ltd in 1933. This edition features all new typesetting and the
illustrations have been re-originated from the German first edition of the book
to give a much sharper, cleaner presentation. The text of the original book is
unchanged and therefore may feature expressions and sensibilities that are at some
distance from what is considered politically correct today.

For a complete list of Casemate titles please contact:

CASEMATE PUBLISHERS (US)
Telephone (610) 853-9131, Fax (610) 853-9146
E-mail: casemate@casematepublishing.com

CASEMATE PUBLISHERS (UK)
Telephone (01865) 241249, Fax (01865) 794449
E-mail: casemate-uk@casematepublishing.co.uk

CONTENTS

LIST OF ILLUSTRATIONS

PREFACE

There will always be war as long as there is life on earth. Individuals will come to blows, quarrels will arise in families. Tribes will have their feuds, nations will fight battles and races will destroy one another.

War will be eternal and stronger than any religion.

Every war has a purpose. Sometimes this is clear enough for everyone to understand it, but often it is quite obscure. The limits of necessity are blurred, and so no one can grasp the purpose of the war.

War has its horrors. Fearful agonies follow in its train. But every war has also its values and beauties. Cowards do not love the battlefield; they tremble, and in their fear they can only see the pettiness. Afterwards they can grumble at the war.

There will be many grumblers, because there are many cowards. But many men took their share in the war. The one served his gun, while another soared in the air and fought honourable duels. A third crouched continually in the trenches and was only an insignificant fraction of the mighty struggle.

Men learnt to know one another in the fire of murderous battles when everything petty fell away from the individual, leaving the spirit naked, pure and devoid of falsehood. Then there was nothing mean or insignificant left; war stood out in all its exalted greatness.

We must all die one day. Every man clings to life. We of the younger generation had our whole lives before us; we had the most to lose.

But Death lost his terrors for us, because he became commonplace and natural. Our fear of Death vanished because we learnt to despise him.

We airmen had the best part of the war allotted to us. We were not exposed to many circumstances that wore down and broke the others.

We still had the honourable combat of man against man, that stood out like a thing of another age amid the din and shock of mass warfare.

And we loved those combats above all else. Because we loved them whole-heartedly, the war became a thing of beauty for us. A set of values was created for us, and we knew nothing else save war. Therefore we found a home in the war.

Chapter 1

FLYING A SCOUT MACHINE

It is raining. A fine but persistent drizzle. Grey mists hang over the valley of the Meuse; the water on the flooded meadows resembles a dull brown mirror, with many cracks and splinters.

We are bored. The Verdun front is quiet. Only very few machines are sent up from our group, and it is always the same story when you have to fly. You hang about in the air for a couple of hours, fly the course set by the observer and feel like a kind of superior taxidriver. Then you lounge in your quarters, nail pictures from illustrated papers on the walls and get really angry when you think of the comrvvades belonging to the Jagdstaffels* who win victory after victory.

I too want to be a scout. But I must wait until my observer goes off for instruction. He put in for a transfer some time ago, but applications must travel long roads, which are often longer than a man's life. We both want to get away—he to a scout school, I to fly a scout. But we have grown used to one another, and I do not

*For the benefit of the layman I must state that there is no translation for the German word 'Staffel,' which signifies a formation of about twelve machines, but is not the equivalent of either our flight or squadron. The Jagdstaffel was a formation of single-seater fighting machines. TRANSLATOR'S NOTE.

want him to have to fly with a strange pilot. Such changes in a team bring little good with them; only too often they lead to a speedy crash.

So I must wait! The whole world around me has lost all semblance of reality. One goes on dreaming, and the grey day seems all the greyer.

At last! My transfer has come.

I execute a joyful dance round the room, which causes Wart, my faithful sheepdog, to open his eyes in astonishment. Then he accompanies my whoops with a series of wild barks.

I must pack my trunk. I must say goodbye. I feel the impulse to be gone. Even though I must leave many good comrades, what is the parting in comparison with the joy of flying a scout machine!

Why am I so delighted?

Life here gains in beauty and variety. Almost every flight is a success. We note the effects of the artillery and feel pleased when we secure a direct hit on a particularly promising target. We bring photos home and endeavour to trace the enemy's recent activities amid the maze of trenches and shell-holes displayed on them. We are as pleased as children at Christmas when a new battery position comes to light. We are helping the infantry, we are wanted everywhere, and from above we survey the full extent of the battlefield. Almost every flight is a success.

And then—there are two of us.

Another human being is partner of my fate. If anything goes wrong with the machine, we are both in trouble. The observer puts his trust in the pilot's flying skill, the pilot in the observer's watchfulness. A single stream of blood flows through the machine from the pilot to the observer and back again. Every danger is shared, and affects both equally. The pilot knows what is coming even before the observer raises an arm to point it out to him. Every brief second is a co-operation, every long hour a mutual endeavour. And yet—something drives me away.

It is no desire for novelty, no grasping out after successes and distinctions. It is my longing for a better machine, better flying and perhaps—for solitude.

It is also the joy of battle.

We had a different goal in our heavy two-seater. The battles we fought were defensive ones, thrust on us by necessity.

But battle is the main objective of the scout. He rejoices in battle, in his attacks,—not in the killing.

He stakes everything on complete victory or defeat.

"Unless you've the courage your life to stake,
That life you never your own can make."

I am seconded to Jagdstaffel School No. 2 in Saultain, near Valenciennes. This is my transition period.

The mess of the Jagdstaffel School is thronged with many strangers, but I meet a few old friends. Many aircraft of varied types stand on the tarmac. I recognise only a few of them by their appearance; they are all new when I come to fly them.

We fly and fly. Short starts, long cross country flights in squadron formation. We loose our machine-guns at ground targets. We go into one turn after another; and so we learn.

The grey wintry sky does not permit high flights, but I utilise every spare moment to put in my requisite number of hours, to finish my course and get away again.

It is not comfortable here. Everyone is thinking of his new Staffel; we remain strangers to one another. Why should we take the trouble to get to know one another better? In a few days we shall all be somewhere else.

At last I am through and have passed my tests. Only a little while more—then I shall be at the front again. It cannot be long; my transfer is perhaps only a matter of hours, or a few short days at the most.

Christmas has come. Another Christmas in the enemy's land. They are getting the mess ready for the feast. I have obtained leave, because I want to be alone. I shall go to Brussels.

The train is supposed to leave Valenciennes at four. I wait at the station. They say the train is late; no one knows how long we shall have to wait. If I leave the station, the train is sure to come, and I shall miss it.

I wander up and down the platform. I shall soon have nothing more to look at; I have read all the notices and stared at all the pictures, but the train does not come. It is very late; night is on us.

At last, at 8 p.m., the train comes along. Well, it is not so far to Brussels; I shall soon be there, with the lights and warmth of the city around me, and I can rejoice in the brightness of life. I climb into a compartment; it is not very clean; the cushions are torn and a window-pane is broken. A cold draught of air circulates through this compartment, but what does it matter? I shall soon be in Brussels.

We start off. In my corner I dream of happy hours. Opposite me sits a lieutenant, sleeping muffled up in his overcoat. We journey onward for an hour. Then the train comes to a stop in open country. It waits a long time; something has gone wrong with the engine, and we must wait for spare parts. It is 10 o'clock; my hopes of a jolly evening fade away. But it is Christmas Eve, and so one expects something special.

I start a conversation with my fellow-traveller; naturally we talk about Christmas. Another Christmas in the enemy's land—how many more there? I ask my companion whereabouts he is stationed, and he replies that he is on home service. He has gone up to the front to get a Christmas present for his mother. He tells me that he is no longer fit for active service, and now I see that one sleeve of his coat is empty.

A Christmas present for his mother? Yes, a couple of coaches ahead lies his dead brother. He has exhumed him and is bringing him home so that he may sleep in native soil. That is perhaps the last Christmas present for an old woman—her dead son. My companion grows silent. He has been spared to his mother—a part of him at least—mutilated and broken in health.

Christmas night—silence.

A cold wind sweeps into the window and makes me shiver. The train starts off again, and the wheels beat time on the rails once more.

We reach Brussels at midnight. A huge decorated Christmas tree stands in the waiting room, blazing with many lights. Silently I take leave of my fellow-traveller and trudge off to a hotel. But everything is shut now; there is nothing more to eat and drink. Somewhere I creep into a strange, cold bed.

Chapter *II*

WITH JAGDSTAFFEL XXXIV
ON THE VERDUN FRONT

VERDUN again!

My new Staffel is quartered at Chenois, near Virton, which is not far from my former unit. I greet old friends, and the world laughs once more. With outstretched arms I gaze up into the blue sky that will soon receive me again. At last I am a scout!

My first visit is to the new machine. A Pfalz D.3 stands silverlike in the hangar. I stroke the cockpit and play on the bracing-wires that sing like violin strings. My identification marks are painted on the machine—a lilac stripe behind the seat and a lilac coat for the propeller bonnet.

Soon we shall take off.

I have made my quarters habitable, and now I have no further desire, save to fly again. I do not think of home any more, and in my delight I have almost forgotten the war.

My first start.

Three of us fly to the front. There is not much to do; we are the only aircraft to be seen far and wide. The old, familiar country-side glides away beneath me. There are clouds high above me. Isolated anti-aircraft shells ascend to us and stand out as dark points against the clouds. The sun gleams on my wings; often I stroke the machine parts about me and pat the silver skin of my plane—just as I used to pat my horse.

Homeward once more. Swiftly I dive into a thick cumulus cloud and leap over soft edges of cloudlets and refuse to believe that I must land. That is how a young steed should feel when he first emerges from the dark stable to the summer pasturage.

We flew every day, and my pleasure remained undiminished. I played with my machine and danced through the air and took no thought of the world around me, until one day a giant's cold arm grasped out after my life and the smiling domain of the sun was darkened by the shadow of war.

The three of us were flying to the front at a great height. I was on the left, somewhat above my Staffel-leader. Suddenly several distant machines came into sight.

Slowly we draw near to them. A broad, two-engined Caudron shoots up before us, and we make a joyous onslaught on him. Then I catch sight of a French scout, almost vertically above me. He is flying in the same direction as we are, and so appears to be almost standing still. I can study his machine at my leisure; its cockpit is painted black, with a huge white skull on one side, while the red, white and blue cockades shine in the blue sky. I am as pleased at this vision of beauty as I should be at the sight of a dragon-fly gliding past my boat on a lake.

Suddenly I see the Frenchman rear up and loop; the next moment his machine-guns are rattling away behind me. I go into a turn at once, but my opponent is sitting on my neck all the time, and soon his bullets hit my machine. A violent blow on the shoulder pushes me down in my seat, and for a brief space my machine goes into a spin. I catch it again, but the rattling continues behind me as I go into turn after turn. Petrol squirts out round my legs, and my petrol 'clock' tells me I have lost a lot of juice. At last the firing stops; I try to take my bearings and find I am a long way in the enemy's country. I go into another turn and start off homewards, but once again the machine guns rattle away behind me.

My petrol is finished. I switch on the emergency tank—thank heaven, it is still full—and fly northwards in zigzags.

I do not care whether I am shot down or not, but at least I mean to reach the lines so as to avoid falling into the enemy's hands.

The rattle behind me continues at intervals, but I see no more of my opponent and notice no more hits on my machine. At last I am over the lines; there is a light wind behind me, carrying me home, and so I reach the aerodrome on my last drop of petrol. Happy, though still dazed from the incessant turns, I examine my machine. Sixteen hits altogether, two of them in the pretrol tank—they might easily have proved fatal. One bullet shot away my safety belt at the shoulder, and another carried away its fastening to the seat. And then I suddenly get the explanation of that continuous rattling behind me. The ends of the belt swung out, and the metal fastener which should have kept them together across my chest kept banging against the cockpit, thus creating the illusion of machine-gun fire in my excited mind.

I laughed, but felt ashamed and learnt a big lesson from that fight, because I realised that I had nearly fallen a victim to the greenhorn's innocence and carelessness. The first weeks in a Jagdstaffel are always the most dangerous. There is so much that is new and unusual that one often forgets to pay the necessary attention. Either one is flying over new country and spends too much time looking down to find landmarks or else the machine is unusual, and too much of one's time is taken up in flying it. An old, experienced opponent notices these troubles only too easily; he only needs to make a sudden attack to be sure of his victim.

I knew the country and had survived a number of fights in my old unit; moreover I had got accustomed to flying the new machine. And yet I was taken completely by surprise. It was my period of initiation, which everyone must pass through, with its accompanying, inevitable perils that either make or break the flier.

All of a sudden I realised the war once more. My play time was finished, and now every flight became a necessity and the fulfilment of duty. Formerly I regarded my guns as a burden on the machine, but now my wings are only there to carry the guns.

Flying is no longer a game, but a matter of fact, and my life has become an onslaught on the foe.

Flight after flight.

The front is quiet; enemy aerial activity is slight. Gradually the ground beneath us changes form; the last snow-flakes have vanished, and the bushes in the Meuse valley gleam up to us with a blood-red hue. The tree-trunks of the Woevre forest no longer stand out against the snow, but merge into the ground, while the sky is reflected from thousands of watery shell-holes. A thousand old shell-holes and a thousand new ones.

The battle down below still goes on.

Up above we do not see much of it; we keep the air free so that our working machines can fly unhindered; we fight our opposite numbers who are in the air for the same purpose.

It is not always easy for us. The French machines seldom show themselves, and often we have to fly a long way behind the enemy's lines to catch an opponent. The Frenchman only fights when he has the advantage of numbers; even then he is not a dashing adversary and soon breaks off the combat. He generally tries to achieve success by surprise attacks.

Archie barks up at us.

The Glassworks Farm with its pentagonal forest clearing vanishes behind my wings. Before us lies Verdun. The sky is clear, except for Archie's shell-bursts at various heights.

Verdun lies below us now. Black and white shell bursts dance around us; they spring up out of nothingness and appear suddenly in front of my nose.

Verdun lies behind us. Douaumont looms up over my right wing. The anti-aircraft barrage becomes thicker. The air-pressure set up by the explosions tears at my wings. Shell-bursts swirl past me like mist. Always new shell-bursts . . . more and more of them.

The sun gleams on the murky waters of the Meuse; a bright ridge shines upward—hill 304.

Anti-aircraft fire at all heights; several splinters catch my wings. Everywhere I see the black and white shell-bursts. Behind us there is a long lane of dissolving cloudlets, a rangefinder for the enemy.

In front of us a grey hill looms up, furrowed and torn—the Mort Homme. Verdun is now far behind us, and the sun is at our backs.

Something flashes above us; a pair of wings flash out, and then another. Two, three, six, twelve machines. At last they have found us. All the Archies cease with one accord. Machine guns hammer and rattle, aeroplanes rear up and circle round—then all is silence once more.

Now I am over the lines. Archie starts again. I look round for my companions and see the Staffel-leader. But the other machine is missing.

We search the countryside.

The shadow of a cloud lies on the field of shell-holes. Between the lines, on the Mort Homme, there lies a broken machine of our Staffel.

We fly homewards. The shell cloudlets have vanished, and in the mist a grey hill is fading away—the Mort Homme.

Our comrade is to be buried. An infantry patrol has found him and brought him back. And so he comes home to the Staffel even in death.

He was hardly twenty four hours with us. He joined us yesterday evening, and at the dinner we gave to welcome him we felt that
we liked him; he fitted in with us so well. This morning he had his
machine assigned to him and was so pleased to see it decorated
with his identification marks. And then he went up into the sky
with the same longing and desire that we all feel.

But then his machine lay broken on the Mort Homme. Not
four and twenty hours since he joined us!

Many officers from the base and neighbouring formations
stand at his grave. The priest's words echo in the silence. Distant
anti-aircraft fire reaches our ears, and a gate of golden clouds shuts
off the evening sky.

I am sitting in a comfortable room. Outside a warm drizzle
flows ceaselessly . . . the spring rain. The odour of the steaming
soil is wafted in to the window, and all buds unfold themselves to
the spring. Mother Earth draws her first deep breath.

Our aerodrome has become a quagmire, in which the wheels
of the machines often sink in up to the axles. Wet clouds hang
down to the ground, veiling the tiniest hillock and disclosing not
even the smallest outlet through which we could creep to the front.

The rain rustles down, and we are at rest.

Life is very gay in the mess, with music and song and games,
and even a bit of guzzling. One can still buy so much in Belgium.
Yesterday we stood ourselves a whole crate of oysters, and now we
sit before our plates, stuffing ourselves like rats in a dug-out. Our
meals are always of excellent quality and well prepared, since we
have acquired a female cook.

A real, proper female cook! That just shows what can happen
in a war!

Many of our younger men had to be transferred from the
Staffel to the infantry. We needed all the rest of them to keep our
machines in order and do the work on the aerodrome. That meant

effecting every possible economy in mess and personal service.

But at the base establishment in Virton there were a number of auxiliary workers, who had been sent out from home, including a few women serving as typists in the offices or assistants in the tailors' shop and stores. So one fine day a person of the female sex came along and offered us her services as cook.

We were all flabbergasted. There was a solemn council of war, with many pros and cons. G.H.Q. could not have given more thought to the decision about a new offensive.

A female cook in a Jagdstaffel!

It is impossible to employ any person of the female sex with a front formation. But on the other hand we were some distance back, and she would be exposed to no more risks than in an office. We therefore decided to give her trial; the negotiations with the base were put through quickly, the transfer from the typist section was arranged, and the cook made a solemn entrance to our Staffel.

She was no longer in her first youth, which was good. She was not pretty, and that was better still. But nevertheless she exercised the best possible influence upon our mess staff. All of a sudden the plates were polished and the cutlery shone; there was not the slightest speck of rust to be seen on any knife. Table-cloths were washed more frequently and grew so clean that it was no longer possible to ascertain the nature of the previous week's gravies. No male on our staff wanted to expose any of his weak points to this woman.

It naturally got about that we were employing a woman. Visitors dropped in on us from all the neighbouring Staffels and groups. Every guest expected something out of the ordinary; before his eyes floated the vision of a dainty figure with fascinating locks and a fancy apron, etc. They were all convinced that the title of cook was merely a cover for something highly improper, and every one of them was disappointed when vouchsafed a glimpse of our good, worthy cook.

The many visitors played havoc with our alcoholic resources. But that was the only drawback, otherwise we were all completely satisfied. Not a single minute did we have to spend in repentance for the new addition to our staff.

Still raining. It has been raining for days.

Little catkins are growing in the meadows, and the first colts-feet are in blossom on the stony hills. A breath of spring lies over the land, and great presentiments possess our souls. Something is going to happen; we are all unconsciously aware of changes to come.

1.3.18. All leave stopped. Censorship of letters. We can still write, but all letters must be read and passed by a censor. Does that mean a big offensive in our part of the world? Or are we down for a transfer? Ideas whirl round in our heads; we discuss all sorts of possibilities in the mess and dream of future successes.

4.3.18. We have orders to hold ourselves in readiness for a transfer. So we are getting away! Our hopes rise to jubilation. We are moving off from Verdun—to a new front—perhaps to a sector where the English are flying—perhaps to the scene of a great offensive—yes, certainly to a great offensive!

And it will be soon. Jagdstaffels are always the last reinforcements to be sent along for an offensive.

Our trunks are packed. Only the fewest necessary machines are left for use. Everything else is stowed away and ready to be loaded up.

We plague our heads with speculations over our new sphere of action. Many fingers run along the map in vain endeavours to define a new flying area for us. The only thing certain is that we are going to get away, and even this is not quite certain. It may all be a hoax.

8.3.18. Correspondence veto. Not a letter or a card may we send. The event is coming nearer and nearer.

Waiting becomes a torture. The last machines are dismantled. Goods trucks collect at the near-by station. A train is put together; perhaps it is for us. We do not believe everything we see; it may only be a hoax.

Wait and hope!

11.3.18. The Staffel is entrained.

Lorries tow the aeroplanes to the siding; ammunition stores and boxes of spare parts disappear into the goods trucks. Our trunks are sent for, and the train is ready to start off sooner than we imagined. We have said all our goodbyes and eaten our final dinner in the base-wallahs' mess. We hardly hear the speeches and good-wishes for our future, for in our minds we are already far away.

Our last ride through the familiar streets. Our tender takes us all down to the platform and then mounts a truck as the very last consignment. We get into our compartments.

A gentle shiver goes through the train. It begins to start; it leaves the station. The lights disappear, and the night hides the landscape from us. The wheels roll on, but we cannot tell where we are going.

The dark night sends us all beautiful dreams.

Chapter *III*
THE AMIENS OFFENSIVE

12.3.18. The next morning brings glorious weather. We wend our way through deep peace, through an untouched land. No shell comes from the front, no propeller whirrs in the air, no troops are to be seen. We have the illusion of being on a holiday trip. We perch in the open air on our cars that are mounted on trucks, and warm ourselves in the sunshine. A glorious landscape flits by us. It is really a holiday trip.

Montmedy, Sedan, Meziéres-Charleville are behind us; the train did not branch off southward. Signs of pleasure become manifest; we are not destined for the Champagne. Soon we must come to the dividing line between the French and English at the front; we shall then know whether we are going to be allowed to fly against the English.

We pass through splendid forests, the outposts of the Ardennes; for a long time the Sormonne stream keeps us company. In a little while the silence becomes almost oppressive, and we are glad to see field-grey soldiers again at a provisioning station.

The provisioning stations are a fine institution. The train stops somewhere; we see huts and a busy life. We get out, sit down at a table and wait for the surprise. Often we get quite a decently cooked meal,—meat and various etceteras,—though often only 'barbed wire entanglement' and bread. But even that tastes good, thanks to the holiday feeling which every train journey brings with it.

Tournes junction lies behind us, and still we go on northward. Hirson comes, then Laon. Slowly and ever more slowly the train rolls onward—to the right. General jubilation; it is now certain we are going to the English front. We do not care where—it is all the same to us now. We hope it will be somewhere right up in the north, near the sea, because it will be pretty country there. But that is unlikely, because it is a quiet sector, where no heavy fighting need be expected. We discuss the possibilities of Y pres, Lille and Valenciennes.

Our train reaches another junction: Avesnes. It goes on northwestward. Gradually we find a busy traffic developing on the rails. We pass the halting points of other transports, while many empty trains meet us on our way.

We reach the big junction of Aulnoye, and our train turns southwestward. That means we are going in the direction of St. Quentin. The evening falls and wraps our further progress in a veil of mystery.

The wheels roll on and on. Our progress becomes slower. The train takes its time round the curves, as though tired of what it must drag—onward, ever onward.

Other trains follow us; we meet more of them at the stations. Like dark serpents they writhe along all the lines, with their interiors full of men, beasts, guns, arms and men again—for the offensive. Hardly a light shows in any of them; they grope forward like black fingers, toward their unknown goals—to the big push.

We cannot sleep. Our eyes scan the darkness in quest of something certain.

The train runs into Le Cateau station. All lights are extinguished. We wait for hours at a siding.

The gleam of a pocket-lamp gropes its way to our coach: Orders: detrain here.

Le Cateau? So it is here, then?

GERMAN BIPLANE OVER VERDUN DEFENDING HIMSELF
AGAINST AN ATTACKING FRENCH SINGLE-SEAT FIGHTER.

LANDING AT OUR NEW AIRFIELD AT FOUCAUCOURT WAS
DIFFICULT BECAUSE OF ALL THE SHELL CRATERS.

Shaded lights illumine the long platform. Train after train pushes its way along and halts. We see cannon and yet more cannon, men and yet more men.

An adjutant is waiting to take us to the new aerodrome. It is a field stretching far away to westward, with mists swirling mysteriously about every depression in the ground.

13.3.18. It is going to start in a few days. We are allowed to rest until it does. We must not fly for fear of giving away the secret.

Our hangars lie scattered in the protection of the trees. We assemble our machines, while yonder on the nearby railway line trains roll up. An uninterrupted procession of trains rolls on towards the west.

17.3.18. Three Jagdstaffels are collected on our aerodrome. The machines are ready to start, but as we have not yet received orders to fly, we must sit quiet while everywhere around us the excitement rises to fever-heat. Artillery rumbles through the lanes, light cannon, heavy mortars,—and then the infantry.

But at night—only at night.

Wraithlike, the endless columns wind along the roads. A lamp shines up . . . "Lights out! Lights out!" Nothing must be given away to the enemy. Columns, always fresh columns. Here a marching song rises to heaven and dies away in the distance, there a military band urges the feet joyously forward, yonder drums and fifes resound. But the basic note of all this music is the rustle, crunch and tramp of countless feet.

Night by night this goes on.

English reconnaisance machines push forward to us. Parachute lights flutter down from the dark sky and illumine the roads over a wide area. Then all traffic stops, and the troops crouch lifeless under the shelter of trees and houses. Nothing must be given away.

By day strong squadrons of enemy bombers range far into our hinterland. I stand at the telescope and follow their flight accurately. Two, five, seven machines. They are coming over to us; their path is lined with many shell-bursts. Further back there is a German Staffel somewhere in the haze. If only I could be up with it!

Our Staffel approaches; its machines grow larger to the eye. Soon they will be within range. The English turn away, but one of their machines lags behind—now an Albatros is on it—a short fight, and the enemy falls. The machine crashes not far from our aerodrome, and we rush off to it.

We find the remains of a huge bomber, The observer is dead. The pilot is crushed to death by the engine. The broken red, white and blue cockade stares up from the green of the meadow. And close to it we find the first spring flowers, the first violets—it is spring.

18.3.18. My friend Riedle, an old regimental comrade, is with Staffel 16. We are glad to meet again; we talk over old times in the regiment and hope to be working together up aloft soon.

At last we are allowed to fly, but only over the aerodrome. The weather is glorious—real spring weather.

The English come over to bomb us every day about noon. We shall be waiting for them to-day.

The Staffels start.

We are two thousand metres up. At last the shell-bursts make their appearance at the front and grow thicker in our direction. That means the enemy is coming. Black dots detach themselves from the blue of heaven. The English are flying at a great height—well above us. We are too deep, but Staffel 16, which is the only one to be flying at practically the same height as the enemy, attacks him. There is a wild fight above our heads, but we can only look on idly. I recgonise the identification marks of the individual machines quite clearly and see a Sopwith attacking the Albatros with the black hearts painted on it—my friend's device. The Albatros flies on calmly— the Sopwith attacks again—the Albatros goes down in a steep dive.

Is he hit? No, surely not. He is flying too steadily although the dive is very steep. I lose sight of him.

But Riedle did not come back that night.

OBSERVER WAVES THANKS AND FAREWELL TO
THE PROTECTION OF THE SQUADRON.

We have found Riedle's machine; it had bored its way deep into a soft, damp meadow. Riedle, mortally shot through the head, was buried underneath it. Another friend gone!

How often we rode out together on the eastern front! We came back unscathed from a number of patrols, but we were not fated to fly together. He lies dead before me, wearing his Uhlan tunic, and on his wrist there gleams a dainty gold chain.

In the night before his death he told me about it, and about a woman whom he loved very dearly.

20.3.18. Our infantry still march frontward in endless columns, regiment after regiment, with transport trains and lorries between them. No rest the whole night long; always this roaring and surging, like the approach of a thunderstorm.

A LONG LINE OF SINGLE-SEATERS FROM JASTAS 35 AND 23
STAND READY AT THE AIRFIELD AT EPINON.

Tomorrow is to be the great day—the day of the onslaught. Tomorrow everything will be merged into one vast battle; blood will flow and victories will be won.

Tomorrow, perhaps, I too shall be dead.

21.3.18. I wake up with a start. It is just after two o'clock; a gentle shiver goes through the house, a dull, continuous roll drones on my ear, a monotonous keynote, broken by louder beats — so loud that they set the window-panes resounding, while the furniture and utensils in the room vibrate from their force.

The drum fire has begun. I cannot sleep any more; my mind is over-wakeful, strung up by the coming events.

Dawn finds us all at the aerodrome. The engines have done their trial revs, the machines stand in long rows, ready to start. No one speaks a word; with ears turned westward in the grey twilight we all listen intently.

Slowly it grows brighter, but with the daylight comes a mist. We must wait idly. The mist spreads and grows thicker.

Hour after hour goes by; the fire from the front grows fainter, because it is muffled by the white wall of mist. Here and there it seems to have died down altogether.

9.30 a.m. Now the infantry is advancing to storm. But we must still wait here.

At last a faint ray breaks through the mist. The sun fights his way through and sends a beam across the silver cockpits of our machines. The coloured devices on the pilots' seats shine brightly. Nothing can stop us now.

The mist breaks, and we start. Three Staffels take off against the enemy.

The canal bend at Bellenglise shines up. That is where the old positions were; the earth steams and smokes from a thousand shell holes.

A deep layer of haze spoils the distant view. We circle round behind the English positions. Very few enemy aircraft about. We have a scrap with four Sopwiths, then with two, and again with another couple. But these English machines soon break off and vanish in the haze. We took them for hardier foemen, but possibly the uncertainty of what is happening on the ground has an injurious effect on their flying activities.

After a little while we can find no more enemies in the air. We fly in wide circles over the scene of the onslaught. Our petrol runs low. I have to land at another aerodrome to fill up for the journey home.

Back to Le Cateau. Then forward again. We sense the hurry of the moment, the forward movement on all roads, the thrust . . . We are through—the first line is won.

Below us a battery is firing, infantry are advancing to storm. Columns take cover in trenches and behind rising ground. Everywhere I see flashes—smoking, flaming mouths of the cannon . . .

22.3.18. Mist again, thicker than yesterday. Not until the afternoon does it yield to the sun.

Our cars bring us to the aerodrome. We pass infantry columns, that still march in endless ranks, we pass the first groups of English prisoners, flowing in ever-increasing numbers from the west. Then more infantry marching into action with bands playing.

The English are in retreat. Very few enemy aircraft at the front.

The second defences have been carried all along the line. We are proud to be German soldiers.

23.3.18. The offensive goes on. The third line falls. The weather is splendid; not so misty as yesterday. We get clear distant views.

We fly forward. Peronne is burning. The smoke of many conflagrations rises up. We find no adversaries in the heights, so we drop down, often as low as one hundred metres from the ground. Below us English artillery is in retreat, khaki infantry hastens westward. Many brown figures lies scattered on the ground, lifeless.

We fly over Peronne. My engine seizes up and will only work spasmodically. I must turn back. The Verey lights I fired as signals pass unnoticed in the smoke. I must go back to the front alone. All around me is the smoke of the burning town, and so I lose my direction.

Suddenly two machines jump up before me . . . Engish two-seaters. They attack me. I cannot rely on my engine now, but I mean to sell my life as dearly as possible and so attack one of the Englishmen. A couple of shots—gun jammed—yes, it would at such a moment. I feel myself defenceless, and in my rage I try to ram an enemy's machine. One of the Englishmen has lost height in a turn; I bear down on him, my fingers press the trigger-buttons, and suddenly the guns begin to fire again. Then I see the observer in the other machine collapse and his pilot lurch forward. I pull my stick hard and just get past the English machine, which goes down on to its nose and falls vertically. It crashes in old shell-hole country amid the ruins of Barleux.

The other Englishman breaks off the combat and vanishes in the mist. I make an effort to find my way, trying to steer an eastward course by my compass. My engine runs worse and worse, but at last I see the front, with field-grey soldiers below me once more. My petrol is nearly done; below me is shell-hole country, which is far from suitable for an emergency landing. I carry on; at last a wide field extends before me, an aerodrome. I land on the last drop of petrol and find myself at Villers-le-sec. That means I have drifted a long way southward. The mechanics of Jagdstaffel 79 attend to my machine, and then I start off home.

All is well in Le Cateau, where I report my first victory. Everyone in high spirits, as the Staffel has scored quite a number of successes to-day.

My first! I often pictured to myself how it was going to happen, but it was a quicker business than I could have thought, and quite unexpected. It was really a fluke—quite unintentional—so that I cannot honestly be proud of it.

24.3.18. The offensive is still going on. Quite a lot of territory has been gained already; the enemy is throwing his last reserves into the fray. His flying formations have shifted their aerodromes to the rear, and now they are quite ready to fight again. The air resistance increases. We meet large groups of them, and every flight brings stiff tussles.

The weather still keeps fine. The murky waters of the Somme flow through the shell-torn land, which is rent and ripped anew before its old wounds have scabbed. At the crossing near Brie we see a number of tanks that have got stuck here. Below us lie the deserted English aerodromes of Mons and Estrées; the hangars which the swift retreat left them no time to destroy completely gape upward in their loneliness with wide, black jaws.

Machines are swimming all about the air. Most of them are German reconnaissance machines, with groups of scouts here and there. Several enemy squadrons hover in the sky, with wings that gleam in the sun.

Gradually a formation approaches us. It is higher than us, and with the sun in our eyes we cannot tell whether it belongs to friend or foe. Now those machines are above us, and we spot their cockades in the sunshine. We close up and await their attack.

A Verey light shines out on high and sinks towards us with long trails of smoke—the signal to attack, given by the English leader. They dive down on us, and already they are in our midst.

Turn, turn, turn, high and low. Tracer bullets cleave the air. Machine guns rattle everywhere, engines roar, bracing-wires groan and howl in dives.

We are flying a big merry-go-round, one behind the other, so that we cover one another's tails. I see a Sopwith attack the Albatros in front of me and shoot at him sideways. He breaks away and goes into a turn to escape. Our turns grow narrower and narrower; my sights follow his fuselage, and it looks as if my machine guns were joined on to his tail. My tracer bullets skim along the edge of his fuselage, but again and again he pulls himself out of my sights.

At last I get on the mark—a hit—petrol squirts out of the machine and hangs in a long streamer of haze from its tail. The Englishman is hit and goes down in a spin. I have no time to follow him down, because I am attacked at once.

Turns, turns, turns, turns,

Everywhere the rattle of guns. The air is thick with the threads of tracers, which are torn by propellers and twisted into all sorts of shapes by propeller-winds.

Turns, turns, turns, turns.

Another English formation joins the dogfight, which becomes fiercer than ever.

Turns, turns, turns, turns.

I am standing still in space, and the world is going round me in crazy circles. Then I turn, and the world stands still.

An Englishman goes past me in a spin, to crash somewhere down below.

Turn, turn again and shoot.

Another Englishman goes down.

The fight still continues. I have lost all ideas of time and space.

The English break away, and suddenly we are alone again. The quiet is something incredible. We muster; I count our machines. None are missing. We have lost a lot of height through our turns. Down below I can see two English machines, while a third lies not far away on the slope descending to the Somme—my victim.

We land on the deserted Estrées aerodrome. All of us are safe and sound. There are a few bullet-holes in our wings and cockpits, but they are just the ordinary results of any air-fight.

Our flight was a great success. In spite of the enemy's numerical superiority we suffered no losses and scored three victories.

28.3.18. The battle is still going on. The artillery fire sounds more distant every day, and the flight to the front grows longer.

We move up to a new aerodrome, at Bouvincourt.

The village lies in the midst of territory that was long fought over; often enough has the din of battle raged round its walls. Most of the buildings are in ruins, but all over the place we find English corrugated iron huts, some in good condition, others gutted and smashed. Our quarters and mess are in a house that is fairly well preserved. It has even got a roof, but its interior is gutted, and all windows have gone.

Our plundering expeditions in the vicinity meet with much success. We find ever so many things that the English had to leave behind because they were in such a hurry: beds, furniture, blankets, stoves, coal, petroleum and even a piano. Vast supplies of munitions are stacked up tidily near the rails of a narrow-gauge railway. The barrels of heavy guns are lifted to heaven. Light guns lie deserted everywhere, singly and in batteries. Round every one of them there are heaps of shells.

We possess ourselves of English rifles and try our hands at

target practice on the English munition dumps, whereby we often raise a pretty display of fireworks.

By evening we have made things quite cosy in the empty rooms. Someone plays the piano; by the light of a petroleum lamp the rest of us read the English illustrated papers we find lying about in large quantities.

29.3.18. Bad weather to-day. Clouds at all heights. A storm. We fly all the same, because the duty machines have to go forward.

Snow at eight hundred metres. We therefore stay quite low and have a scrap with a few English machines. The rain whips against one's goggles; gusts toss the machine up and down; one is so busy trying to manage it that one has no time to look at what is going on below. Through the swirls of mist the earth assumes a spectral appearance as it flits away beneath us.

30.3.18. The English have dug themselves in. To-day our people are attacking at Hamelet.

Gloomy weather again; getting worse and worse. But what does the weather matter? We just fly.

We start and land on a battle landing-ground close behind the lines. All quiet in front of us—only a few stray shells drone across. The clouds thicken and drop lower; a thin drizzle falls earthward.

At last we can get off. In a trice we are over the lines. And now the artillery fire starts. It rolls and booms; despite the roar of the engine I can hear every explosion. Trails of smoke stream upward everywhere. Groups of infantry work their way towards the enemy's positions, batteries thunder away. Flying quite low, we behold the battle as a huge spectacle.

English observation machines streak off as we approach. As the air is now clear, we take a hand in the battle down below by shooting up nests of snipers and artillery positions. Khaki figures crouch anxiously against the sides of their trenches, pale faces that stare up at us look like distorted masks. On we go. At one gun the whole crew duck behind the shield, at another they run off into a trench, but one fellow sinks to his knees and throws up his arms to heaven. On we go! Heavy infantry and machine gun fire pelts up at us, and holes begin to appear in our wings. But what does that matter? Carry on!

Now English fighting machines make their appearance. They flit like shadows through the shreds of clouds and try to attack our infantry. They are not going to succeed, because we are there—so they turn about and sheer off.

The rain becomes thicker; it whips against the skin like hail. Goggles are continually getting dimmed, but carry on! A Sopwith hurtles out of a cloud in front of me; he sees me and goes into a turn, but for a moment he stands quite still in the middle of it. I take aim—shoot—my tracers hiss across to him in long threads and eat their way into his fuselage—a red flame jets out—wing over wing the Englishman goes down in flames—my third! But I have no time to waste thought on him—carry on! Fresh enemies come, vanish and come again, while below us the battle thunders and roars.

31.3.18. Easter Sunday. The sun has forced his way through. Easter rises in the radiance of a sunny morning. A silvery sheen bedecks the countryside. I think of home and the mountains; I see the new snow sparkling, I see the deep green pine woods. My eye seeks the little lakes which reflect the distant meadows.

Far away there lies a fair land. My home land. Now the church bells will be ringing as the peasants go home in their gala dresses. All the gentians in the dewy grass have liquid pearls in their calices. Laughing eyes rejoice in the world which is so beautiful to-day. Home—home!

Our home is the war. We know no other. We are a wheel in a vast mechanism.

We are still young, but our childhood lies far, far behind us. Far away, with our youth, lie our homes and the times of peace.

We have grown old and found a new home—the Jagdstaffel. Our lives, all our thoughts and feelings belong to it.

We have grown lonely. We are only a little group of men who belong to one another. We share the dangers of the front, we are a part of the great battles, but we do not belong to the front.

We are lonely. Generally we are quartered at the base; we enjoy the pleasant life of the base, but we are not part of it.

We are lonely. Everyone of us went forth with some regiment to defend the homeland. We left our country and then we left our regiments, to find loneliness and a new home.

What do the others know of the beauty of loneliness, of the splendour of our new home!

We must be lonely, because we possess the most beautiful of all things—flight and the combat in the air.

All around us lies dead land—ruins that have been thrice levelled to the ground. New shell-holes, with brown pools that reflect the blue of heaven, are born beside the old ones that are choked up and overgrown with grass. Far and wide there is nothing but dead land—ruins and wreckage.

Here was once a pleasure-garden . . . Stunted green things are growing amid the burnt debris.

A white star! In the morning sunshine the first butterfly sways gently on a daffodil.

4.4.18. Rain—rain. The drops patter on our sheet-iron roof, and make sweet music in my ear. To-day we can rest. It does one good to snuggle up in the bedclothes and sleep . . . sleep.

The telephone growls in the corner. There is an attack going on to-day; the English have sent up a number of fighting squadrons and we must come to the rescue. What a damnable invention is the telephone!

So out of my warm bed and away to the aerodrome! We cast imploring glances at the heaven which refuses to relent—the rain still goes on.

We are in the air, and it is not so bad as we thought. So over the lines once more, with the old landscape rolling away below us.

But we cannot keep together, for patches of mist make it impossible for us to see even our immediate surroundings. Below us the heavy guns thunder and rifles rattle.

An English machine flies out of a cloud and passes quite close by me. The next moment it has vanished again. I try to cut it off and scour the grey haze from which it is bound to emerge.

Now its cockades reappear. The English pilot keeps his machine calmly on a straight course; the observer does not notice me because he is concentrating all his efforts on searching the ground below. My guns give fire; the English machine goes on to its back and then drops. I have great difficulty in following its progress down through the haze, but see it crash in a little wood.

Another Englishman flies at me—clouds—mist—I change my course by turning in a cloud.

In front of me I see several machines of our Staffel, and further away some more English ones. The conglomeration of clouds grows thicker; we fly eastward and are compelled to land on another Staffel's aerodrome as we have lost our direction. Then we go home.

Another call for help comes just after we have landed. Our wings are quite soft, our propellers all rough and ragged, but no matter—we must take off again.

It is raining in torrents when we start. The haze is so thick over the front that the Staffel gets lost at once. Sometimes I see one or other of our machines, but that is all. The eddies caused by the artillery combine with the tempest to tear at our wing-tips; around me clouds seethe as they mingle with the smoke and dust sent up from the ground.

Suddenly I find an Englishman quite near me. I make for him, and our turns in the clouds bring us so close to each other that our wings are almost touching.

Now he is in my sight. I shoot him down in flames. The flames glow weirdly against the grey of the clouds as the machine falls to the black earth like a huge fireball.

Several other English scouts try to catch me, but I take speedy refuge in a thick cloud. I am quite low down when I emerge from the haze, but the clouds are hanging down to within twenty metres of the ground. I go nearly over on to a wingtip to dodge a big poplar, and then I have to hop over all sorts of obstacles such as houses and avenues of trees.

I shoot down the big road that leads eastward. Now I am over a village—it must be Warfusée. Its streets are thronged with troops, who wave up to me.

Darkness falls apace.

17.4.18. Spring marches deeper and deeper into the land. The rains of the last few days have conjured up fresh greenery everywhere; violets and anemones bloom by the hedges, primroses cover the field of shell-holes. A peach-tree by a broken house-wall has burst out into masses of pink blossom.

Nature pursues her eternal round, untroubled by the activities of mankind.

Black and white cloud-horses gallop across the sky, a few thick raindrops pelt down, the storm rushes into the branches of the peach-tree and whirls blossom petals aloft.

Then all is quiet once more. Patches of sunlight flit across the young grass, chivying one another. More and more of them follow, until all at once the whole countryside is one vast blaze of sunshine and laughs and laughs—laughs itself into intoxication from the spring air and laughs at mankind.

22.4.18. A new aerodrome has been found for us. It is much nearer the front, on the huge straight road and close to Foucaucourt. We migrate thither; one after the other, our various accessories are brought up from Bouvincourt, and the removal is soon finished.

The Bavarian Jagdstaffel, No. 77, lies next to us, while a Prussian Jagdstaffel occupies the other end of the ground. We are not far from Cappy, the headquarters of Richthofen's squadron. At first we find our starts and landings on the new ground rather difficult because of the numerous shell-holes on its surface. Our aerodrome squads have their hands full filling in the holes and trenches.

We are living in a desert. Not a house to be seen anywhere. Many villages have completely disappeared. The only signs of them are boards at wayside crosses on which is inscribed in English: "This was Villers Carbone! This was Vendelles!" Crosses that mark the grave of a whole village.

The buildings were reduced to ruins by shell-fire, the stones and beams were taken for dug-outs. Now these are smashed up too. Often enough the artillery has passed over the land like a gigantic plough, turning up everything and bringing to the surface what was buried underneath. Everywhere I see new and old graves. There are crosses on the slopes, in the hollows and in long trenches. These graves mark the places where the battle laid low the men who sleep in them.

These graves are particularly thick along the great road where close and distant fire combined to deal mortal wounds. Many of the older crosses lie on the ground, decayed, overgrown with weeds; the names they bore are obliterated and forgotten. Old, rusted barbed wire winds its way up the hill. Every cross on a French grave bears a red, white and blue cockade, put together with tin and paper. But these are all rusted and torn; the cockades stare up like tired, wounded eyes from the gloomy grey-brown of the field of graves.

My memories go back to Russia. There was a great road which led to the front. Often and often we passed along it to our position; often and often our columns trod its surface, which was sand in summer and a deep morass in winter and spring. Along the side of this road lay bodies of dead horses, a body to every metre of road, and in the particularly bad spots the horses lay heaped on one another, sprawling out on to the road, where they were trodden into the mire. There were too many of them to be counted. Poor horses, what did you know of the purpose of your death?

We live in the midst of this field of graves. But the war has accustomed us to sharing our home with the dead.

Near the aerodrome there is a small wood of beeches and alders. We have cut a way through its wild undergrowth and put up our tents and corrugated iron huts in its midst.

Twelve of us inhabit one hut. Our beds stand in rows; we stumble over trunks and twist our devious ways past our neighbours. This does not worry us so much, because we can always behave in neighbourly fashion, but our animals are not quite so amenable.

Some of us have dogs, one owns a cat, another has brought three magpies along, while yet another has caught a fox-cub. All this menagerie has to be parked in the one hut, over and under the beds, thus curtailing the space available for the humans. Unfortunately all the dogs are at war with one another in addition to cherishing the most evil intentions towards the cat. The latter lies in ambush for the magpies, with the result that we often arrive home in the middle of a scrap and just in time to prevent a tragedy. The fox-cub is the only one that sits good and quiet in his corner, but he gets so bored that he goes and grabs everyone's boots in turn and gnaws them. Owing to the presence of the aforesaid menagerie the air in our hut is not exactly what one would call pure ozone.

Thank the Lord, the weather is good, so that we can spend the greater part of the day in the open air. We have a lot of flying every day, and in the evening we are so tired that we do not care where we sleep.

23.4.18. We have suffered a great loss! Richthofen is dead! Yesterday we were flying as usual in our Amiens sector; Richthofen's triplane Staffel was at the front at the same time. There were a number of encounters; we saw the other Staffel having a dogfight with some English machines. A 'tripe' went after an Englishman, followed him right down and then landed suddenly between two shellholes behind the English lines.

That evening we learnt that Richthofen did not come back. Richthofen taken prisoner a great loss—but at least he was alive. Perhaps he got a shot in his engine, but we felt sure he must be unwounded because the 'tripe' landed. It would be impossible to put this machine smoothly down,—in shell-hole ground too—if the pilot was badly wounded.

But to-day we heard Richthofen was dead. We would not believe it at first; we thought it was a false report issued by the enemy. But now it is certain.

Richthofen dead! We whisper the dread tidings softly to one another; our laughter dies away in the mess. The hammers are silent in the workshops, the engine that was just being given its trial stands still. A gloomy silence broods over all.

A great one has gone from us. In the midst of his successes after a record number of victories, he found a swift and happy death when leading his Staffel.

Oh God of Battles, you can often let men die happy deaths!

Clouds bank up—huge white pillars.

Two ravens, birds of Odin, fly aloft and vanish in the high, blue vault.

The great offensive has come to a standstill. Gradually hostilities are assuming the form of trench warfare again. The new front line runs close to Amiens; the trenches are dug in territory that has remained untouched by the war. We have passed the vast wasted Somme area.

We hoped to establish our new aerodrome further forward, in this new country, but alas, we must remain in the wilderness.

The enemy has developed strength; everywhere there is lively flying activity shown by many squadrons. We fly our old machines as often as we can; we win victories and suffer losses. The English have new machines with which they can fly at great heights, unattainable to us. At five thousand metres our machines are uncertain swimmers and sideslip in their turns.

With envious eyes we see the Fokker triplanes of the Richthofen Staffels rise up playfully above us and haul their victims down from the heights.

But we are in the air as often as we can manage it—for what else can we do!

Chapter IV

MAY 1918 IN THE SOMME AREA

<hr />

L ife is somewhat boring, because we get so little variety in our wilderness. But the return to trench warfare brings one good thing with it—leave. Everyone of us can fly to Brussels in turn.

Out of the desert into a town of light and splendour—it is like a fairytale.

A small suitcase is stowed away in the machine; the wheels taxi and take off with the nose pointing northeast instead of in the direction of the front. The shell-hole field grows smaller, the Somme disappears, great forests show up as dark patches on the landscape. The country becomes more thickly populated, village abuts on village, stacks of coal rise like pyramids from the ground, great red industrial towns stretch fingers of chimneys to heaven. In the distance a huge mass of haze rises up, and in front of it I see a broad band of forest land, with shimmering castles. From out of the haze gleams a golden dome—Brussels.

I land at Evère on a beautiful aerodrome. The machine goes into the vast airship shed, where it looks quite a dwarf. My feet tread paved paths. A tram takes me into the centre of the town.

My first visit is to a hotel. The Palace Hotel at the station. It is very difficult to get a room here; they are all reserved for the quality—persons with or above the rank of major. But you can cultivate good relations with the hall-porter, who is susceptible to a substantial tip as well as being not particularly well disposed towards the higher ranks.

A room with a private bathroom. A bath is the best and most beautiful thing of the whole war, and when one has vegetated a bit in this part of the world, a hot bath in a proper bathroom is doubly good. I lounge away a couple of hours in my bath until the life-urge tugs at my stomach to warn me that it is time to think of other matters. I don clean underclothes, slacks and patent leather boots; then, newborn, I descend the stairs to the diningroom.

Outwardly as pure as a candidate for confirmation should be in his mind, but with an unsuspicious soul I step gently into the salle à manger. I look round for a table and overlook a general standing in the doorway; he addresses me in gruff tones. I apologise; the general wants to say all sorts of things to me, but I steer a course to my table, leaving him alone in his glory.

I sink into a soft armchair; a white tablecloth, shimmering china ware and silver cutlery smile at me. It is all so different from the meals out there. The headwaiter brings me something to eat and drink. I swill down oysters and close my eyes in bliss.

A fat uniformed stomach, with many coloured ribbons and a general's shoulder straps, comes up to my table and takes me to task for my uniform. Apparently I am not dressed as the regulations prescribe.

He is quite right on that point. My tunic collar is turned down, and I am wearing a soft shirt-collar and a tie. We have adopted this custom from the English, not to be fashionable or funny or even to annoy generals, but because it is very practical. A closed tunic-collar worries one's neck when one has to turn one's head in all directions during a flight. A soft collar is healthier and more comfortable.

The general demands that I shall remove my collar and tie. I explain their purpose and assure him that I am going to take them off when I go to bed. The general blows up in rage. I am not worried; I give my name and the number of my Staffel and request the decorated stomach to either take a seat at my table or else let me have further particulars in writing. Being all for peace and quiet here, I then sit down again and continue my meal.

The general retires with a face as red as the stripes on his trousers, telling me I shall hear further about the matter.

Generals do not love airmen, as a rule. But even the oldest general fails to make an impression on the youngest lieutenant in the air service. Most especially not, if he is a general at the base.

I leave the hotel happy and replete. Evening descends, wreathing the town in delicate blue veils. Lamps shine out; shop windows are illuminated. It is like wandering in an enchanted land.

I meet an acquaintance and stroll with him through the streets, through this shimmering unreality.

And what a lot of things there are here! Meat, sausages, white bread and cakes in the shops, even flowers—but what have we to do with flowers in wartime? We have heard a lot about food shortage in Belgium—well, there does not look to be any shortage here.

Oh, what a lot of nice things! Girls laugh at us, and we speak to them. Yes, the world may condemn them and eye them scornfully—but we find pleasure in them. They are cleanly dressed and make a pleasant change from the eternal field-grey.

We are young; we want to live, and tomorrow we shall be dead. We have nothing but the war; no women await our coming, for our home is the Staffel.

Let the philistines at home wax indignant if they will. We do not care; in any case they can never understand us. We are young; we want to live, and tomorrow we shall be dead. You little girls of Flanders, we thank you for many happy hours, the memory of which is more precious to us than the unctuous sermons of world-reformers, whose words are only empty noise.

Life laughs at us from a thousand eyes.

We go from one place of entertainment to another. Music greets us everywhere; here a good string band, there the squeaking pipes of an orchestrion. They all sing to us a song of life. Wine bubbles in our glasses, girls dance . . . music and light and life.

The next day I make a few purchases, and then a quick flight takes me back to the Staffel. The fair countryside vanishes, the first Archie shell-bursts shoot up in the distance—the front has me again.

At last we too are going to get better machines—Fokker Triplanes. It is true that they are discarded machines of Jagdgeschwader and therefore contain quite a lot of hidden snags, but that does not diminish our joy. Three of them have already turned up. There is great competition as to who is to fly them, and finally we let the dice decide who shall be the first and in what order the others shall have their turns.

At first we find these new machines a bit strange to fly. But they are extremely sensitive to the controls and rise up in the air like a lift. You climb a few hundred metres in the twinkling of a second and can then go round and round one spot like a top. The rotary engine takes some learning before you can manage it, and is rather a difficult business at first. But it is not long before we are all at home on them, and everyone wants to be flying a 'tripe' when an English bombing squadron comes across. But just at present the bombers are off the map and confine their activities to night shows.

19.5.18. Whitsunday. A bright blue sky, streaked with a few summer clouds. Nothing special during the front patrol. Nothing much doing to-day.

We are flying back to the aerodrome, when suddenly we see three English two-seaters lower than ourselves, with an escort of five machines above our heads. They are coming from our hinterland and streaking for the front. We fly towards them; a strange joy sets our propellers whirring fast, and soon we reach them. Now our leader's machine dives down on the Englishmen below us, and just then the bunch over our heads descends on us, so we take them on. They are two-seaters, Bristol Fighters, and we are amazed to see how nimble they are. A wild dogfight begins, but the odds are on our side because we are over German territory and there is a slight breeze which drifts us further eastward. The fight splits up into groups; everyone has found an opponent and will not let him go. Our Staffel-leader has already crippled his adversary and follows him down, I then see another Englishman being fought down. Meanwhile I go on turning with my man, but suddenly the observer stops shooting, and the machine goes down in spirals. This Englishman seems to want to land, but as it may be a trick I follow him down and take care not to let him out of my sights. But he drops deeper; now comes a last turn, the machine flattens out makes a good landing on a field, taxis and comes to a stop.

It sits there on the grass like a big butterfly, with its cockades shining gaily and peacefully.

I send a couple of shots in its direction to make sure that its crew get out quickly and refrain from destroying the machine. But men hasten up from an adjacent camp, and soon the Englishman is surrounded by a crowd of them—the enemy's capture is assured. However I have known our people damage a machine from pure stupidity and therefore land on the same field. I can hardly wait till my machine has stopped taxying, but at last I reach the vanquished foeman.

It is a strange spectacle: a thing that I have been fighting, a thing that was turning its guns on me, a thing I could hardly see at all in the hustle of our turns—and now it stands quite quietly before me.

The pilot, an English lieutenant, is lifted out of his seat; he has a bullet in the upper part of the thigh. The gunner, a sergeant, is unwounded. Both look very unhappy, but their faces brighten up when they catch sight of me. It is rather an unpleasant business to fall into the hands of the troops; they are not very kindly disposed towards enemy airmen, especially if they have ust had a few bombs dropped on their huts. And so the two Englishmen are delighted to see a German airman come along.

We greet one another almost like old acquaintances. We bear no malice against one another. We fight each other, but both parties have a chance to win or lose.

In a kind of a way we are one big family, even if we scrap with one another and kill one another. We meet at the front, we get to know the respective badges of Staffel and Squadron and are pleased to meet these old acquaintances in the flesh.

The fight is over, and we are good friends.

For the present the two Englishmen are taken to a near-by hut, and I have a close look at the captured machine. A beautiful new thing. What a profusion of brass and rubber there is about it! The enemy can stand himself such luxuries. Poor Germany! It is a long time since anyone has seen a sign of brass about our machines, while the aircraft at home and in the flying schools have to economise with wooden wheels.

Its wings are painted a beautiful, smooth, even ochre; it has flat bracing wires which make such a funny ping when you touch them—a bright note with a soft echo. It makes lovely music now; when those wires sing to us from the heights at night, they sound more unpleasant, especially when there is a bass accompaniment of a couple of bomb detonations. But I am delighted to get the machine intact. Some pilots are of the opinion that a victory is only complete when the other machine goes down in flames, but I prefer to capture it uninjured. Likewise I prefer living prisoners to dead foemen. But unfortunately one cannot always arrange things as one likes; sometimes they turn out one way and sometimes the other.

I put a guard over the machine and start off home. A hop over a little wood and a bit of a field, and I am there. The Englishman came down near Proyart, which is quite close to our aerodrome.

I return at once in a car to fetch the wounded pilot. He is happy to get to a dressing station so quickly. There is a hospital close to the aerodrome where we know some of the doctors; we take the Englishman there, and soon he is receiving the very best attention.

We fly the English machine to our aerodrome. It is not long before it reposes peacefully in a tent. Our little scouting machines surround it, seeming to gape and snuffle at it like village curs around some dog of strange, rare breed that has lost his way.

The day draws to an end. Its strong colours grow dim. The sky becomes a vast expanse of opal and then fades into softer tones. A mild, warm May evening lies over the land. Rest and deep silence. Not a single shot comes from the front; they all want to make holiday there.

Our beech hedge is decked with young greenery. Through the dusk of evening Chinese lanterns glow in the branches. A cockchafer hums in the air . . . softly, lest he disturb the stillness of the twilight. We sit at a long table under the Chinese lanterns. The Maybowl sparkles in our wide glasses, and we rejoice in the lovely evening. From a distant tent belonging to our men the strains of a gramophone are wafted across . . . peace, peace.

The night is on us; stars twinkle through the foliage. Pearls of dew glitter like rare precious stones in the coloured light.

From afar comes a low drone, which grows louder and heavier. A German bomber flies low over our heads and passes on towards the front. It flits across the night sky like a shadow, and its exhaust glows like a spectral eye. Thus the war warns us of its presence.

23.5.18. The leader of Jagdstaffel 77 fell in an air fight. His body will be sent home.

A tent-hangar stands open wide; its vast interior shows black against the sky. In this tent lies the coffin. Two scout machines stand as silent sentinels about the catafalque.

Young May greenery rustles in the gentle breeze.

A priest speaks solemn words. Funeral music resounds over the aerodrome.

The coffin is born on the shoulders of comrades from the Staffel. Slowly the procession begins to move. For the last time the leader crosses his aerodrome. Round the car his comrades say their last farewell to the dead; then he starts his long journey homeward.

We stand there with bowed heads and clenched hands. We have little to say to one another, for we know that our destiny is the same. It may come soon, it may come later.

The spring heaven laughs in radiant blue. From near and far we hear the songs of propellers. Shrapnel clouds line the horizon. The war goes on and drags us out to combat.

Our lives are long, because our experiences are so manifold. Death is short and swift in the airy heights.

We are permitted to fly so long in the light and sun, and our death-fall is so short.

Only the body sinks into the grave.

28.5.18. I have been appointed acting leader of Jagdstaffel 77. Now I must command a Staffel, direct attacks and bear the responsibility for men and machines. I am proud that this is permitted me.

I shall not lose my old friends because the new Staffel is at the same aerodrome. The comrades of the new Staffel are not strangers; we have been acquainted with one another for some little time now.

Mist rises up in the Somme valley and thickens into clouds. My Staffel takes off. One after another the machines circle round the aerodrome until the last of them has left the ground. It is my first start as Staffel-leader.

The other machines muster round me and fall into their flight positions. We fly frontwards in close order. Six machines behind me. I keep on counting them and wave to my nearest neighbour. None of my previous flights were so beautiful as this one.

Deep below us there is a belt of haze. Thunderstorm clouds pile themselves up into gigantic towers. Visibility is bad to-day.

Five English machines are circling over the lines, at long distances from one another. Apparantly they are spotting for their artillery. I try to encompass them and force them over our side of the lines, but they divine my intentions and retreat.

A battery of Archies sends some shots in our direction. They do not bother us because the clouds make accurate marksmanship impossible. Like birds of prey we slink along the edge of a big cloud.

Suddenly I see an Englishman before me. I dive—a quick glance round at my Staffel, all of whom are diving behind me— then my machine guns begin to shoot. The English machine makes a feeble turn, goes down in steep spirals and crashes on the edge of a wood southwest of Gentelles.

We fly homewards, along the round masses of cloud that grow thicker at all heights. I wave gleefully to my six followers. My first flight with my own Staffel has brought me a victory.

1.6.18. Front activity as usual. We had flown one patrol to-day and were just about to start off to the front again when the telephone rang. An English raid was expected, we were told. We stood by for further orders.

Through the telephone comes the news of strong enemy aircraft activity. The Jagdstaffels receive orders to fly barrage patrols along the front.

I take off with my Staffel and fly at a height between four and five thousand metres along our sector. Ground and westerly visibility are very bad; the evening haze hangs round the ground like a thick veil. Further away to the south we see Archie's shell-bursts, stretching away to eastwards, where an English formation is flying to its work.

Specks in front detach themselves from the sky and approach us. Twelve English two-seaters pass above us, flying at six thousand metres. Shell-bursts hang round them and follow them eastward.

Another English squadron comes along—twenty heavy machines, with about the same number of scouts flying above them. They also fly over our heads, taking hardly any notice of us. They do not stop to attack us because they are carrying heavy bombs to drop in our hinterland or going on a photographic reconnaissance.

We are supposed to fly a barrage patrol and prevent any English machine passing over the front. We therefore pull our machines up, but fail to rise much higher than five thousand metres. The enemy remains out of reach; we can only send a curse after him.

More squadrons come.

At last one approaches at our height. Scouts. They attack us. The turns begin. Wings gleam everywhere, and the phosphorus ammunition cuts white threads through the air. We have no losses and no victories. We lose height; my altimeter shows only four thousand metres, but the English break off the fight.

Another English formation attacks us. I can count twenty-five machines, and there are ever so many more flying above them. Turns, turns, but my Staffel keeps together, thank heaven. I chase after any single machine I can see, give help wherever possible and defend myself by going into further turns. But whenever I attack an Englishman, there are five others sitting on my neck.

The fight lasts a long time. Again we suffer no losses, but once more we have lost height. We are being forced down a long way behind our lines.

Another English squadron attacks us. I cannot count the machines; there are more and more of them. Strong squadrons are flying over our heads again. Further away to the north another German Staffel hugs the horizon, fighting with a large number of English machines. Their experience will be similar to our own.

The rattle of machine-guns thunders into my ears, and my engine howls in the turns, but I hear practically nothing. An oppressive silence seems to brood over us all. Up and down goes the fight; wings go round in vertical circles, the earth is on top of the sky, which lies right down below. Everywhere the air is full of brown machines with cockades; the grey fuselage of a German is a rarity.

We are in our line of captive balloons. One balloon is burning. We are supposed to be flying a barrage patrol, but we are impotent to carry it out. Two of my machines are missing, and ammunition is running short. We are still eight hundred metres up. Petrol is running short too. We fly in the direction of our aerodrome in order to gain a bit of height. Behind us another balloon collapses in flames; a black pillar of smoke ascends across the red sky of evening.

Not far to the aerodrome now. Again another English squadron comes along and attacks us. We are almost directly over the aerodrome. We are being forced down on to our own aerodrome. We just hang there like discs in the air. Really, it is no use carrying on; we are three against thirty, all going round and round in never-ceasing turns.

A machine belonging to my Staffel rears up and crashes. An S.E.5 comes into my sights; my last bullets hiss against his fuselage. Petrol fumes squirt from his yellow flanks, but I can see no more of him in the turmoil of the fight.

My petrol is finished; my engine stops. I do not need to worry about landing; my wheels come down on the aerodrome; the skid crunches along in the sand. Then all is still—most uncannily still. I wrench the goggles from my face and stand up. There is a silence of death around me.

Propellers drone in the sky. Thunder dies away in the distance. And now I hear our Archies shooting; they have never stopped firing, and the sky is full of black cloudlets.

Mechanics rush up to me and push my machine in the tent. One after another, five machines of our Staffel have landed, all badly shot about, but still serviceable. One machine has crashed, with the pilot shot through the heart. We have also shot one Englishman down.

Taken all round, the day was a success for us, a great success. We were seven, and we fought against something like a hundred. We did not, could not fulfil our task of flying a barrage patrol; seven machines cannot stop a hundred from flying across. For the first time we realise the enemy's enormous numerical superiority.

We can only clench our fists in impotent rage.

Chapter *V*
LEADING JADGSTAFFEL XXXV

1 2.6.18. The general commanding the air service has nominated me leader of Jagdstaffel 35. A former leader who was at home recovering from wounds has returned to the front to take over No 77.

So now I am definitely a Staffel-leader. My new Staffel is in the Cambrai area. I can scarcely wait until I am with it, but in spite of my pleasure it is hard to say farewell to old comrades. One tries to carry it off easily and makes a jovial speech at the farewell dinner; one nods silently to one friend over the glasses and presses the hand of another in silence. We all have our faults, but we have stuck together in good and bad times.

Side by side our machines soared in the air. The colour-stripes on the fuselages look so beautiful and jolly. Generally the white and the bright red were nearest to me, but the blue-white-blue can also tell many tales of flights we shared. There are the two greens, the yellow and the Staffel-leader's double-red. Dear old colours! We stuck together, and now I must leave you!

We laugh and sing, and our tongues tell tall yarns. But my heart enquires timidly how you will all get on when I am gone. When shall I see you all again? Who will be the next to go?

Well, be that as it may!

At last I have a Fokker D VII.

13.6.18. My machine leaps from the ground and pushes up into the clear air. I am not going frontwards to-day, but north-east, to Cambrai and my new Staffel.

The shell-hole territory disappears; the long, straight roads from Bapaume and Arras to Cambrai shine white against the yellow-green of the fields. Bourlon wood slips away below me.

Epinoy looms up. The tents and hangars point the way to the new aerodrome. I land and taxi slowly to the hangars—towards my new destiny.

An officer comes up to my machine. I introduce myself.

"Ah, the new Staffel-leader!" A swift summons goes forth; the pilots collect, the men stand by.

I greet them all. I should have liked best to take off for the front at once, but a heap of work awaits me, and I must get through it first.

Things do not look too good in this Staffel. Three leaders have fallen within a brief space of time. Some of the pilots were wounded; others got themselves transferred to other Staffels. Our machines are old Albatros D.5s and Pfalz D.3s., with not much fighting value. The various squads are the only items that seem to be up to strength.

Where am I going to begin?

My first journey was to the commander of the Air forces attached to the army corps. I explained to him that I could only lead the Staffel if I received full support from the Casualty and Machine Replacement Departments. This was promised me.

My next visit was to the Jagdstaffel schools at Valenciennes and Nivelles, where I chose some new pilots. Even if they are young and inexperienced, they are better than nothing—and better than old, war-weary men.

The machines were put in repair, and the pilots flew themselves in on them. As air activities were not very lively at the time in our sector, I had sufficient opportunity to initiate my new pilots into the ways of the front. And so, within a few days, I was able to lead five machines across the lines.

30.6.18. The work of instruction has made June pass quickly. Now the machinery is at work; one wheel interlocks with another, and everyone is glad to see things running along smoothly.

To-day I had six machines behind me. Hard on my left flies Sergeant Schmidt, on my right Sergeant Prey, two excellent pilots who never budge from my side. Behind them the others, spaced out at due distances at heights.

We are flying along above the Cambrai-Arras road, which is our permanent signpost. Two other straight roads stretch out from Cambrai into the distance, one north-west to Douai, the other south-west to Bapaume. Our sector lies more or less between them.

First we pass over hillocks and valleys, with various little streams; on our right we see the gleaming water of the many lakes of the Palluel area and the lengths and bends of the Sensée Canal, while Bourlon Wood lies on our left. Then the country grows flatter and greyer; I see some big, new shell-holes close to the villages and at the cross-roads. After that the Scarpe gleams up; the last vestige of green vanishes from the soil, which is now a dull grey or brownish-yellow, torn by many shell-holes.

The great, broad, white strip of the road still runs beneath us, but it is smashed and battered in the battle-area. Now it fades away in a mass of haze, to come to an end amid a mass of ruins and debris. Arras lies directly below us; the front line is just in front of the town.

The citadel's star-shaped walls stare up at us. Red flames flash out from its north corner. An anti-aircraft battery is firing.

And now the batteries in the centre of the town must surely join in. Quite right! Here are the first shell-bursts from that direction! We have learnt to know them well enough in the course of

time, even if we have not learnt to love them. If any particular battery did not start firing, we should miss it.

Now the flashes start at St. Catherine. 21,22,23,24—so many
white shell-bursts are already in the air. You people down there will
never learn to shoot, however long this war goes on! Your bursts
are all in the wrong places, far too low and to the side. Well, we don't
mind.

Like Cambrai, Arras is the centre for three great roads which
run out in north-westerly, westerly and south-westerly directions.
But these roads begin badly and then pass on into beautiful, untouched country.

Here and there we see a patch of green land shining in the
distance. Generally there is a thick haze over the sky, while orange-
coloured swathes of mist often mask the immediate view. Visibility
is worst in the evening when the diagonal slant of the sun's rays
causes them to dazzle us more, while the haze sparkles like a mirror.
At that time our reconnaissance machines have a difficult task, and
artillery spotters can hardly find their targets. We scouts are less trou-
bled by these conditions; we see just as much as we want to see.

When one soars high above the haze-belt on clear evenings, a
shimmering, silver ribbon looms into sight. It is a narrow band that
lies just where the sky touches the horizon.

It is the sea.

We gaze into this far, distant brightness, and a great longing
comes over us. The sea is alien to us; we have nothing in common
with it. But that glittering narrow band in the distance allures us like
infinity.

1.7.18. The sky is full of hanging clouds to-day. Visibility is bad.
The only clear view is that which we get vertically below us.

Four English two-seaters are hovering over Arras; apparently
they are spotting for their artillery. They do not appreciate the many
clouds, and when we approach they withdraw further behind their

own lines to guard against a surprise attack. The Archies also find the clouds a hindrance, for they only send a shot in our direction every now and then.

Circling round in the clouds, we start to lay an ambush. Perhaps we may yet succeed in springing a surprise.

Our machines stand out black against the grey and white clouds. Sergeant Schmidt smiles across at me; he appears to be enjoying the flight.

The world has grown small and narrow. We wind our way through the gates of the clouds, fearful lest our wing-tips may touch. Arras comes into view through a hole in the clouds, all dark-blue and green in their shadows; only a few bright walls stand out to our eyes. Veils of mist flit across.

Suddenly a gay cockade appears from out of the grey.

Close to me an English machine emerges from behind a cloud. A two-seater R.E.8; I recognise the type by its short lower wings; the observer is scanning the ground, taking no notice of us.

The Englishman is in my sights. I have his fuselage quite distinctly in them. After a few shots the enemy heels over and goes down in a spin. I follow him down in steep spirals; at about a thousand metres off the ground the R.E. catches itself, and stands still a moment. Then it goes into a fast spin again . . . deeper and deeper until it crashes . . . on a green meadow close to the north-west edge of Arras, hard by the St. Catherine road. Now the Archies bark furiously at us. But their efforts are vain; we are once more in the clouds where they cannot see us. Sergeant Schmidt's face is wreathed in laughter, and he makes his machine perform the maddest aerobatics.

But the home trip is a wild tussle. We hop about in the clouds like fleas in a feather bed. We are near to getting completely lost, for only every now and then do we get a glimpse of the roads below that give us our direction.

5000 METERS BELOW US LIES THE WHITE BAND OF THE SOMME.
FOLLOWING THE LEADER, THE FOKKERS POUNCE
ON THE BRITISH SQUADRON.

6.7.18. My Staffel has really become a Staffel worth looking at, and I am proud of my work. Everything is clean and orderly. All living quarters have been made comfortable.

A big room in a house has been turned into a mess for the N.C.O.s; it was not long in becoming the centre of sprightly life and sociability. Several men were found to be musicians; from these modest beginnings an orchestra came into existence. Band parts were sent from home. The result was not exactly a symphony orchestra, but a very excellent scratch band.

Our own mess was a poverty-stricken room in a peasant's house. It contained only a few desolate pieces of furniture, so that everyone was glad when he could get out of the dismal hole. But now it has been transformed into an aesthetic home for us. The walls have been decorated with a new, clean wash; a nook has been done up in a different colour and forms a jolly smokers' corner when equipped with tables, basket chairs and soft cushions. From the ceiling a hand-wrought hanging-lamp is suspended; on the walls there are chandeliers with silk shades. There is a buffet, a dresser and lots of chairs and tables. Special corners for card-tables and the telephone. Pictures on the walls—not just leaves cut out of an illustrated paper, but proper pictures, framed and under glass.

All this has been achieved at little cost but with much good will. Moreover our crockery, cutlery and table-linen have been repaired and brought up to strength. Our mess waiter has been inspired to remove the black rims from his finger-nails, and is always properly washed and combed when he serves our meals.

Our mess was therefore at the height of its glory, and we arranged a party as a worthy house-warming. We decided on July 4th, as we had no early morning patrol the next day; for the greater embellishment of the festivities we sent an invitation to the nursing sisters in Cambrai.

Then an idiotic order descended on us from above, for the

powers that be chose that day for an inspection of arms. A captain from the staff of the general commanding the air service came to our group of Jagdstaffels to cast his eye over all our arms, and of course he would chose to visit my Staffel on July 4th, the day of the party. The order stated that the presence of the Staffel-leader was desirable, but not essential.

Well, what could happen, I asked myself, and decided to be conspicuous by my absence. So we let our previous arrangements stand.

The captain turned up and was assigned quarters with the group's staff. He arranged to mess with a neighbouring Staffel, but the good folk there did not treat him particularly well; they refused to put themselves out for him in the slightest and avoided his company as much as possible because they looked upon him as an objectionable superior officer.

Two Staffels were inspected; July 4th was the day for our turn. My armoury officer got all the arms ready for inspection and undertook to see the business through.

We had patrols in the morning and early afternoon. I had hardly landed from the afternoon one before I was summoned to the telephone. Our arms were in bad condition, I was informed; many of them were filthy.

Now there was some truth in the accusation. The machine guns were in perfect order, which is the main thing as far as a Jagdstaffel is concerned, but I had not worried myself particularly about the condition of the carbines, and still less about the side-arms. There was never time to look after them properly; besides many of my staff were old men who had no notion how to handle a rifle. It therefore did not seem to me to matter much whether their fire-arms were clean or dirty if they could not shoot; besides I did not want to have them shooting and playing about with the carbines; their job was to keep our engines in order.

The telephone started buzzing again. This time it was the captain, who wanted to speak to me. I had no time for him then and sent a message accordingly. The reply came back that he would like to drop into tea with us and talk things over. For courtesy's sake I could not object to that, and so I arranged to meet him half an hour later.

Then off I went to the mess with my pilots, to arrange things. I opened the door—and beheld the smiling faces of the three nursing sisters! They had got off early in the afternoon and wanted to give us a surprise. So they profited by the lovely weather to walk along to our place. "And I hope we haven't inconvenienced you by turning up a couple of hours too soon."

"Now we're for it," I thought. "The captain will be coming along directly, and the sight of our rusty swords won't have put him in a rosy frame of mind. He's sure to kick up hell when he sees the girls."

"Sisters dear," I suggested, "you'll have to go along to our garden and pick flowers for an hour or so. There are several things we've got to do. Sorry, but you'll have to vanish for an hour."

But it was too late. Through the window I caught sight of the captain striding towards the house, accompanied by our armoury officer.

I go out to meet him. We greet one another. "Very pleased you were able to come to tea with us, sir. We've got some visitors—sisters from a Cambrai hospital. I hope they won't worry you, sir."

The captain registers amazement, which turns to a slight embarassment. Then he asks where he can wash his hands. He combs his hair and gets his tunic brushed, protesting that he is not properly dressed to go out to tea with ladies, etc., etc.

But at last his toilet is completed, and we enter the mess. Introductions; we take our seats; tea is served. The girls go out of their way to be nice to the captain, and it soon turns out that he knows one of them already—he met her somewhere long ago. So the conversation flows merrily on; the captain reveals himself as a most companionable fellow. Outside our windows evening declines into night; tea is over long ago, but our captain shows no signs of budging. Nothing left for me, but to invite him for the evening.

He accepts with pleasure.

All hands help to decorate the table.

The festivities begin. The meal is not very opulent, but it looks more imposing than it is. A cask of beer is broached, and we clink foaming glasses. Then comes the 'bowl'; we empty one bowl after another. The good old gramophone gets to work; the old records with their various cracks run themselves red-hot. The scratch band whoops and squeaks. Tobacco smoke hangs across the room in blue curtains. It is a jolly evening.

The jolliest of all is our captain. He is so happy to be in the company of congenial souls and continually curses that other Staffel which treated him as an objectionable intruder.

The nursing sisters have gone home long ago. It is some hours past midnight, but we still keep filling up our glasses, while the smoke is thick enough to cut with a knife.

Bright morning arrives before we break up the gathering.

Nothing more was said about the condition of our arms, and my Staffel got no worse criticism than the others.

10.7.18. The bigwigs of our army corps were struck by an excellent idea. It is not often, perhaps, that brainwaves visit high military authorities, but this was a really magnificent one.

And so the whole of the live-stock park was shifted to our village. There was ample room for it, because the village had been evacuated of all its inhabitants, and there were plenty of stables available for the animals. The aerodrome and adjacent meadows afforded excellent pasturage.

It was a pleasure to hear all the bleating and lowing that went on around us. Moreover these flocks and herds were not particularly well watched; naturally economy was the order of the day, so that only a few old Landsturm men were told off as shepherds and cowherds.

It was therefore not surprising that a few sheep, calves and pigs lost their way, and, as chance would have it, these good beasts always wandered into our midst. Strangely enough the men always had sumptuous rations on the day after one of these animals took a wrong turn, while our mess cook suddenly served us with appetising dishes from ribs, kidneys, brains, etc.

The more these animals got into the habit of losing their way, the greater was the amount of talk that went on about them, and soon a whole lot of army orders came fluttering down on us from H.Q., all of which were concerned with meat thefts and the way to suppress them. We naturally read these orders and issued our own warnings, but as the men thought much the same as we did about the business, things went on in the same old way. The orderly officer for the day took care never to inspect our tent-hangars in the evening, because these were the places into which the animals always strayed.

But one evening there was suddenly great excitement. The sergeant-major rushed along to me in dismay.

"There's an ox in Tent 3, sir!" he gasped.

"Well? what about it?"

"There's a military policeman turned up, who swears there's an ox missing, and he wants to search the place.

Now we are for it. "Is it a large ox?" I enquire.

"Yes, sir, quite a big chap."

"And in what state?"

"Just been skinned and cleaned out."

"Very well. In ten minutes time I'll come along with the policeman, and I'm not going to see any ox there."

"Very good, sir." Exit.

The military policeman appears and tells his tale. This takes some little time. He finishes up by informing me that he has instructions to search the whole Staffel.

Very well then. I show him round. We visit the kitchen and the men's quarters. Nothing suspicious comes to light.

The policeman then says he must inspect the hangars. So we go along to them. The ten minutes are up.

Tent 1 . . . Nothing.

Tent 2 . . . Nothing.

Tent 3 . . . Nothing. But there is a strong smell of petrol, and some large patches of oil on the ground. Not a sign of any meat.

Then I see an indefinite something lying in a corner. A yellowish-white, hairy object. I hardly dare look at it; it is the ox's skin.

"What's that?" asks the policeman.

I am ready to give up the game, but the mechanic in charge answers boldly and brazenly that it is a pilot's fur overcoat.

So there was not a sign of any ox. The only ox I saw was the military policeman, who jogged off quite contented.

It is a mystery to me how they managed it, because they cut that whole ox up and divided it into small portions for the various messes—all within the space of ten minutes.

But several days later the authorities removed their livestock park somewhere further back, where there was good stabling and pasturage, but no troops—and, above all, no flying men.

That was a great pity.

17.7.18. A Bavarian division has been transferred to our sector. It is billeted in Cambrai.

It contains a number of old friends, and I visit them to chat about old times. I meet a number of schoolfriends for the first time since the beginning of the war. When I was with the cavalry division on the eastern front, our six regiments were generally working alone or with non-Bavarian units; when I transferred to the Air

Force I found myself always chained to the aerodrome, and so lost touch with other troops.

We sat together at a corner table in our mess—Rainer of the infantry, Manz the sapper, Luber of the field artillery, Kraus of the heavy guns and I, the flying man. We were all only seventeen years old when we joined up, young and enthusiastic. Now we sat together silently; no one wanted to say anything. Everyone of us has had many experiences in those four years—too many. Everything is changed, and yet nothing is changed.

And so our words take a long time in forming themselves into sentences.

The infantryman tells of the trenches. He always goes the same way through mud and mire to the frontline, to his dug-out, no matter whether his sector is Y pres, the Champagne or Arras. The few interruptions when his division is sent to the Carpathians or Italy are almost like holiday trips.

The sapper has the same tale to tell.

War has become just a matter of course to both of them. Life is nothing but a series of trenches, dug-outs, marches and rest billets. There are many objectionable and repulsive features in this life of theirs, but one feeling predominates over all others and helps them across all difficulties. It is the comradeship.

The infantryman is not alone. To his left and right in the trenches are neighbours who feel the same as he does. At his side marches a friend, who talks to him, laughs with him and curses with him when both stumble over the same obstacle. If they are lucky, the same shell finishes them both off. There is always the friend and neighbour for the infantryman.

The two artillerymen do not tell a very different story. Their guns are in the trenches or behind them—sometimes nearer to the front line, sometimes further away from it. Otherwise they sing the same old song of trenches, dug-outs, marches and rest billets.

But the artillery are better off than the infantry. They have their comrades at their sides—and their horses as well. The animal is a far better and truer friend than the man.

You only need to put out your hand when riding to feel the soft skin and the warm life that is linked with your own. The horse's head is always giving you friendly nods; the two ears are pricked up to catch your lightest words. You artillerymen are well off, because you have your comrades and your animals.

And I? I must also tell my tale.

Naturally we airmen see everything. We wander far and wide; we hold converse with those in the highest authority. Yes, I can tell them that. Like the other arms, we have our battles. Our chances of death are the same as elsewhere, perhaps greater because in addition to the ordinary risks of war we have to face the element and the malignity of machines. But we are much better off in some ways. We generally have comfortable quarters and a sure supply of good food. We can wash ourselves and even get baths. Our uniforms are not caked with mud, but neat and clean.

Nevertheless we are lonely. We are just a few men who hold together and are firmly bound to one another. But when we fly, there is always a wide stretch of air between our machines, an infinity.

There is no one above us. Beneath us there is a distant land, the earth to which we no longer belong. For us it is as far to home as to the stars.

Our voices echo in space.

Around and about you there is cold metal and a machine which you control. You learn to feel with it, so that the slightest irregular sound proceeding from it is a roar in your brain. You have grown one in body and soul with your machine, and yet it remains cold and aloof to you—cold metal.

The flier lives in infinite isolation . . .

This isolation is fearful and splendid.

We cannot do without this isolation. We have no desire to do without it. Isolation changes the nature of man, and so many things have changed for us . . . battle, life and death.

Nations wage war on one another. On the earth beneath us men tear each other to pieces. We have our part in the war, and yet it seems that everything that happens below is alien to us. We hover twixt heaven and earth.

We have not attained heaven, and yet we no longer belong to the earth. We are lonely.

Five old schoolfriends are telling each other their experiences. All have lived through many things.

Four years of war, and still it goes on. What will be the end of it all?

Things no longer look well in the homeland. At the front our men are making every possible effort to hold out against an over-powerful foeman—often in vain. Here we lose a trench, there a sector. Slowly our front line is being forced back.

Each of us speculates on the coming end. We do not talk of our homes; likewise we do not ask when we shall meet again. It is war.

Some of us will meet again one day and talk over old times. One of us will say. "Do you remember that so-and-so was alive when we met at Cambrai in July? And so-and-so wasn't dead either then."

But perhaps none of us will be able to meet the others. But it will not matter. It is war.

20.7.18. It has become quite quiet at the front. An eerie silence broods over the trenches. It is quite a rarity to see a shell burst. Our Marne offensive has failed. The planned attack in Flanders has been postponed and cancelled.

The war is pausing for a while to draw breath. In the west a mighty thunderstorm is brewing. We cannot tell where it will discharge its fury. Everywhere I sense the signs of this coming storm.

Enemy aircraft activities have varied considerably of late. Sometimes there was not a single machine to be seen at the front, some-times strong defensive patrols were flying at all heights, sometimes numerous enemy squadrons push deep into our hinterland.

Every day we carried on with our usual patrols. If we found no foemen in the air, we dropped down to shoot up trenches and other objectives and destroy lines of approach. At any rate this was activity of a sort, and so we were satisfied.

At other times we had dogfights with enemy squadrons which were superior to us in numbers and flew better machines. But there was a purpose in these tactics, because the English could do no damage elsewhere as long as they were scrapping with us. They were prevented from molesting our infantry and bombing our battery positions.

But when we had to chase after bombing squadrons, we found the proceedings senseless and unsatisfactory. The English always flew at great heights, never less than five thousand metres. We could never reach this height in our bad machines.

Archie's shell-bursts showed us the enemy's course. If we were lucky, we reached him somewhere in our hinterland or cut him off on his way home. We hung on behind his squadrons and heard the roar of their many engines pass over our heads. Just a dive, then pull the stick, and up you go till you get an opponent in your sights—a couple of shots—and then down you go again because the machine has lost too much way by the climb. This process we repeated again and again, but none of us achieved any success with it. It would have been pure chance if we had.

The climber was the target of all the English observers, who were pleased to test their machine-guns on us. Their bullets rattled about our ears; the tracer lines danced through our wings and round our cockpits. Occasionally a scout came down and made an attempt to engage us, but he generally limited himself to a burst or two and then withdrew to safety in the heights.

The squadrons roared with pride on their homeward way. We remained below in the haze of our own Archies and had all our trouble for nothing. What did it matter if we came home with holes in our machines. We had not done any good.

Several of the neighbouring Staffels were better off. They flew quick-climbing triplanes or the new Fokker D.8, the flying capacity of which was something almost like a fairy tale. They always hauled down one or two from the English squadrons and put the rest out of their stride. But even they did not really do much.

Even when their successes were striking, they were nullified by the enemy's numerical superiority. What is the use of shooting down five out of fifty machines! The other forty five will photograph and bomb as much as they want.

The enemy's material superiority was making itself more and more felt, and so dooming us to failure. The impossibility of achieving anything substantial in spite of all our honest efforts was the most demoralising thing we experienced in the whole war.

The uniformity of my reports at this time paint their own picture of our plight.

5.7.18.	Weather:	Good
	Visibility:	Good
	Enemy aircraft activity:	None
	Enemy anti-aircraft activity:	Lively
	Fights:	None. Lt. Stoer attacked a captive balloon at Anzin.
6.7.18.	Weather:	Clouds at 1,000 metres and haze.
	Visibility:	Mediocre
	Enemy aircraft activity:	Very strong. Barrage patrols at great heights. Working machines with strong scout escorts at the front.

	Enemy anti-aircraft activity:	Slight.
	Fights:	Eight engagements with single and double seaters north of Arras.
7.7.18.	Weather:	Cloud ceiling at 1,000 metres and haze.
	Visibility:	Bad
	Enemy aircraft activity:	None
	Enemy anti-aircraft activity:	Lively
	Fights:	None. Shot up trenches near Arras.
8.7.18.	The same as yesterday:	
9.7.18.	Weather:	Clouds at 1,000 metres. Clear over front
	Visibility:	Very good
	Enemy aircraft activity:	Very lively. Scouts flying barrage patrols at all heights. Working machines with strong scout escorts at the front.
	Enemy anti-aircraft activity:	Weak
	Fights:	Three fights with double-seaters
10.7.18.	Weather:	Rain
	Visibility:	Very bad
	Enemy aircraft activity:	No machines at the front
	Enemy anti-aircraft activity:	Weak
	Fights:	None
11.7.18.	Weather:	Cloudy
	Visibility:	Bad
	Enemy aircraft activity:	Two double-seaters at the front
	Enemy anti-aircraft activity:	Slight
	Fights:	An R.E.8 shot down. Seen to crash east of Roclincourt.

17.7.18.	Weather:	Thunderstorms, clouds, local rain
	Visibility:	Good
	Enemy aircraft activity:	Slight. Five double-seaters over and north & south of Arras at 2, 000 metres.
	Enemy anti-aircraft activity:	Very strong
	Special remarks:	New anti-aircraft batteries identified. One battery of six guns firing N.E. of Arras between river and road bend. One battery of four guns firing in centre of Agny. Shot up first battery with machine guns from 500 metres.
18.7.18.	Weather:	Clouds at all heights
	Visibility:	Good
	Enemy aircraft activity:	Slight. Three double seaters far behind the lines. Two of them seen to land on Files campferme aerodrome.
	Enemy anti-aircraft activity:	Very strong
	Special remarks:	Shot up anti-aircraft battery N.E. of Arras with machine-guns.
19.7.18.	Weather:	Clearing up
	Visibility:	Very good
	Enemy aircraft activity:	Slight. Three double-seaters and five scouts far behind the lines.
	Enemy anti-aircraft activity:	Very strong
	Special remarks:	Shot up anti-aircraft battery N.E. Arras with machine guns. Strong railway traffic (eleven trains) on line Frevin-Aubigny-St. Pol.

Reconnaissances do not form part of our jobs, but whenever we see anything worth while, we naturally report it. The many trains and their white trails of smoke were clearly visible, and in the clear moisture- impregnated air we could follow their progress far behind the lines. There is something important going on over there.

The weather is mending; the sky is clear and cloudless. The bombing squadrons are starting again. The first came across at 9 a.m. this morning, the second followed at 10.45 a.m. Both were making for Douai. We attacked them, but could not reach them on account of the height at which they flew.

We were hardly out of the air to-day. We just came down to take fresh supplies of petrol and ammunition and swallow a mouthful or two. Then we were up again in the hope of catching something. But all in vain.

All our hinterland was full of Archie's shell-bursts. The veil that hung over the towns, stations and munition dumps was particularly thick. On the whole not much damage was done, but the demoralising effect was great. The only good point about it is that the fellows at the base get something dropped down on their heads instead of the front line men. The English have been using every scrap of fine weather in the daytime for their bombing raids—and lately they have been coming over at night too.

They lead us a dance the whole night long. Archies fire away, machine-cannon bark, machine guns go tack-tack-tack. Every transport column is equipped with machine guns and blazes away all over the place, while search-lights grope over the sky and bright star-shells stumble over clouds and wander about, streaking past one another until they fizzle out and flicker up again. Archie batteries from far and near are shooting hard. You cannot hear the distant ones; you can only see their shell-bursts flashing out in orange flames on the horizon and then dying down. Softly to our ears comes the distant rustle of the propellers and the far, clear song of the English bracing wires. The propellers and engines do not sound very different from the German ones, but the tune of the bracing wires is quite distinct.

We stand on the aerodrome, hoping that our ground machine-guns will get a shot at a low-flying plane.

Altogether it is a splendid firework display in a warm summer night.

The night of 22.7.18. Our first night scouting flight. We are to try scouting flights at night. Our machines are not equipped for them, as they lack the necessary instruments. Therefore we must rely on our sensing powers. But these will not let us down; flying has become so much part of our natures that we fly as automatically as we walk or swim.

There is still, however, much to discuss and arrange. These flights are to take place on the bright nights of the full moon; we must have some sort of visibility, for it is impossible to recognise and fight the enemy in complete darkness. I contrive to get the area bounded by the main roads from Cambrai to Arras and Douai and a line drawn between them from Villers-Cagni-court to Aubigny-au-Bac allotted to me as my hunting-ground.

This is more or less a large triangle, defined by plainly visible lines, since to east and south of us we have the big, straight roads while the brooks and lakes give us our north-western limits. This area is not to be flown by any other German machines during my flight, as otherwise they would run the risk of being attacked by me because it is impossible to recognise nationality markings at night and very difficult to spot even the types of machines. I must also have an understanding with the Archie batteries and searchlights in this area,

It was suggested that I should identify my machine to them by firing a white light. We rejected this idea, firstly because the enemy could easily fire a similar light and secondly because the signal would

betray my presence to him. I proposed a sound signal; if I am fired
on by our Archies or caught by our searchlights, I shall throttle down
and open out my engine three times. The men below will hear this
as three successive buzzes, which should answer the purpose sufficiently.

To-day I take off for our first trial.

It is a glorious summer night. The disc of the full moon sits
high in the heavens, pouring a flood of silvery light over the whole
countryside. Crickets are chirping, fieldmice bustle busily to and
fro. From near-by ponds rises the thousand-throated chorus of the
frogs' concert.

Far away to westward a few red flashes streak out—solitary
shells, the bursts of which do not trouble our ears.

In some parts of our area I see the range-finding shots of
Archie batteries rising heavenwards. They ascend on high like shimmering pearls and then die away. To north of me one pearl—a
pause—a second and third pearl. Southward, by Marquion, five
pearls. The low drone of a multi-engined machine rises and dies
away to southward. A German bomber is going off to work.

A searchlight awakes, describes a radiant circle in the sky and
then fades out again.

Now an Archie battery to westward begins to fire; four searchlights shoot up and scour the heavens. The beams of three of them
meet and fasten on to some indefinite object, with which they wander slowly eastward. Several Archies are firing away; soon the beams
of the searchlights are dotted with quivering sparks.

The English are coming over. I take my seat in my machine
and give the "all clear" signal.

I open the throttle. Dewy blades of grass hiss under my wheels,
the engine roars away in the night. The field below me swims out
of sight.

A deep silence. My engine swallows all other noises. I cannot hear the shells of the Archies or the hammering of the machine guns. I am alone, with an engine, a blue night and a great, bright disc of a moon.

I gain height quickly and circle round my area. The countryside below me is a pale grey; it gives a blurred effect, and yet I can distinguish details quite well. With no lights showing, the various villages show up as lifeless masses. The roads shimmer as bright grey lines. The black patch over yonder is Bourlon Wood. Immediately below, dark and dead, lies my aerodrome at Epinoy.

Searchlights and shell-bursts wander up to me. I scour round for the enemy, but fail to find him. The magic fires pass between me and the moon on an eastward course. I scan the milky heaven for a silhouette, but find none.

Suddenly all is quiet once more. The searchlights are dimmed, and no shell-bursts dance in the sky. One beam still gropes about in my vicinity; now it catches me. A blinding brightness shoots into my machine. The wings gleam and glitter. I throttle down three times; the signal is understood. The light vanishes, and once again I am enveloped in blackest night. Only very gradually do my dazzled eyes regain the power of sight.

Blue, cold lonely night. I illumine the altimeter with my pocketlamp. Two thousand metres.

The moon has grown huge, the earth quite small. My sector has become a tiny angle. The Paluel lakes are no longer black, dead holes, but white, glittering precious stones when the moonbeams catch them. I shut off my engine and go down in a slow glide.

The blue light is like a lake in which my machine is swimming. This lake is the silent loneliness of a distant world.

No more Archies, no more searchlights. The only light that comes up towards me is from the range-finding shots of the machine-gun anti-aircraft batteries.

Slowly I sink deeper; the dark land rises up warm to meet me.

Epinoy is below me once more. My light-signal flames out; its stars shiver in the night. The landing lights below burn up in answer to my signal. Two green, one red.

One more turn. The ground below grows uncannily bigger. The green lights flash past on either side of me, my wheels touch the earth, rebound slightly and then come down again to taxi on quietly towards the red light.

The landing lights go out. My machine is wheeled into the hangar, and deep silence broods over the aerodrome once more. The crickets have ceased to chirp; the only sound is the occasional croak of a frog in one of the ponds.

My comrades of the Staffel have followed the whole flight from the aerodrome. It was easier for them to locate the positions of the machines up aloft because they had the assistance of their ears. They tell me that I was often quite near to the enemy. This is little consolation for me, but, after all, it was the first trial, and next time I shall manage the business better.

22.7.18. Bombing squadrons flew over us at great heights again. Impossible to reach them. The old story. 24.7.18. Weather: cloudy. Haze. Visibility: bad.

Enemy aircraft activity: medium.

Enemy anti-aircraft activity: very lively.

Three fights. Heavy firing on positions at and to the south of Courcelles.

The enemy is beginning his offensive. Only partial attacks, here and there, to mask the main blow. Otherwise the front is quite quiet. These attacks are the first gusts of the coming stormwind. The storm will soon begin.

25.7.18. Weather: fine, light clouds locally. Visibility: very good.

Enemy aircraft activity: very lively.

Impossible to reach the strong squadrons that came over on account of their height. Are we to give up hope

At last the news arrives that our scout group is to get the new Fokker D.8s. Either the authorities have realised that we cannot do anything more with the old machines or else the output at the factories has improved. In either case our troubles are over.

At last, at last the Fokkers! But only a few of them have turned up at the park as yet. The neighbouring Staffel has got those few. But our hopes endure and make flying a thing of joy once more.

Several days ago two horses were assigned to the Staffel. So that we can save petrol. Please don't laugh.

Almost every day our people have to go to Cambrai or some dump in the neighbourhood to fetch all sorts of things—petrol, munitions, stores, rations, equipment, etc. For this purpose we send off lorries and so consume petrol. In future the motive power is to be supplied by these horses.

Naturally the order is idiotic. We consume nearly one thousand litres of petrol every day that ten machines of the Staffel fly two hours. Further quantities are used for trial runs and cleaning the engines. What difference does the daily ten or twenty litres for a lorry make? Especially when you consider the loss of time occasioned by using the horses.

Moreover our two horses came from an equine hospital and were so lean and tired that they could only just manage their trudge to the Staffel. They were not fit to work, so we rigged them up a cosy stable and let them graze on the aerodrome all day.

We reported a saving of four litres a day, whereat there was much joy in high quarters. Our lorries went off on their daily journeys, as before, and the most pleased of all were the horses, who thus gained a nice haven of rest after all their war labours. Holy St. Bureaucratius!

We never hit it off well with the base. This was only natural, as the contrasts were too great. The base-wallahs always waged war against us with the pettiest weapons and never stopped trying to hit at us.

The latest effort was a complaint to the O.C. Aviation that we went to the theatre in Cambrai too often. This report touched a sore point—petrol economy. It was urged that we ought not to use this precious liquid for our jaunts if it was so scarce.

The complaint was passed on to me for my official cognizance. I replied that pilots and men required some entertainment in order to keep their spirits up to scratch for fighting and working purposes, and that visits to the theatre were a very suitable means of achieving the desired result. Moreover these establishments were known as 'front theatres,' and we were therefore of the opinion that the men at the front had more right to use them than the base units.

That settled the matter officially, but it was only natural for us to show the base-wallahs how little we were impressed by their complaints. So on the next theatre evening I ordered the Staffel to attend the performance. The neighbouring Staffels were only too glad to join in. On the night of the show the theatre square was one large car park. Wherever one looked, one saw cars belonging to flying groups.

The theatre was packed long before the performance began. Our men occupied the stalls and circles; we pilots crowded into the boxes. Just before the curtain went up the gentlemen of the base arrived, all neatly brushed and ironed, and wanted their usual seats. Anger and astonishment were clearly painted on their faces, but not one seat was given up to them. When a few of them voiced their complaints, fierce mutterings resounded through the whole auditorium.

The base gave up the battle as lost. A frantic round of applause accompanied their exit.

The performance began, and went off splendidly. There was no need to say anything about the contact that ought to exist between actors and audience, because every member of the latter took part in the show.

Afterwards we thought we would like a drink in the base officers' mess. We were prepared for a row, because we knew the gentlemen of the base were out for revenge. But we did not worry about that, as we were just in a nice mood for a scrap.

We entered the mess and—as we might have expected—every seat was taken. Angry faces stared at us. It looked as if we could do nothing but clear off.

Then came help from above. An English bomber visited Cambrai and dropped his compliments. Bang! down came the first bomb somewhere in the neighbourhood—the base leapt up from their seats and made a rush for the door—to vanish into the cellars reserved for such heroes.

Once again the battlefield was ours. We made ourselves comfortable at the vacant tables; soon we were all merry and bright, and the fun reached its height when the actors came along and joined in. What did we worry about the bomb thrower! We took him for a considerate fellow, and if it was fated to be, why then his bombs would find their mark even in the deepest subterranean refuge. I have known a bomb go right through a whole house and burst in the cellar.

Our fun waxed faster and yet more furious.

The good Englishman dropped a few more bombs here and there. So the base did not show their noses, preferring to remain safe in their holes.

But soon afterwards our friction with the base-wallahs ceased because the threatening English offensive and the planned withdrawal of our front line caused the authorities to move the base further back. Thus they vanished from our sight for a little while.

It is now hot summer. The sun burns down from a clear sky, and the air flickers and quivers on our broad aerodrome. Our machines sway and dance in the sun-eddies, and one hardly notices any cooling off even at great heights. Our existence is quite heavenly. When we are supposed to be standing by, we lie naked on the grass and let the sun tan our skins. If an order to take off comes along, we just get into flying kit and go up. I often wonder what the enemy would think if he brought one of us down behind his lines and found nothing but bare facts when the combinations were removed. It would give the Entente journalists material for a fine article about the clothing shortage in Germany!

When we are off duty, we make off as quickly as we can to bathe in the Paluel lakes. There we find rest and recreation combined. Then we lounge about the aerodrome again or go to sleep under the shade of a tree.

Sleep is a greater necessity for the airman than food. Sleep is the food of the nerves. How much time we have often frittered away uselessly with cards, talking and the like. Flying makes a bigger call on nervous energy than any other form of work. You cannot fly well if you do not sleep well.

The currants are ripe in the gardens; they hang like chubby red grapes amid their foliage. Gooseberries are an excellent dessert in the mess, and strawberries float in many a bowl.

The air flickers; a hot breeze comes from the west. The evening sun has set in a yellow layer of heat-haze. From the east evening rises over the land, cloaking the horizon with delicate blue veils.

Away to eastward there lies a far land.

Mountains and lakes and vast forests of fir-trees.

Far, so far away.

I do not think of it any more; it is just a presentiment that rises in my heart. A feeling back for the past, a faint memory of childhood's days, a melancholy yearning.

That land is home.

Shall I see it again? My home is the Staffel.

I want to see the old home again. Just once more.

I want to see it in the setting sun when the mountain glow and the lakes gleam and the blue veils of evening descend.

Once more.

When?

1.8.18. It is about 1 p.m. We are sitting in the mess, just about to go off for the afternoon patrol. Suddenly we hear a roar and a crash; the next moment bombs come down and machine-guns begin to fire. The English are raiding our aerodrome.

We rush out and see the air full of a wild medley of English machines. About twenty of them have come down to one thousand metres to drop their bombs, while a good way below them some thirty scouts are peppering our hangars with machine-guns and hand-grenades.

The attack was planned and carried out down to the last detail. Some of the scouts circled round the hangars and shot them up with incendiary bullets. Several of our machines that stood ready on the tarmac blazed up at once. Other scouts shot up our quarters and dugouts. Yet others hung over our machine-gun Archies and looked after them. It was impossible to fire those guns; if any of us made the slightest effort to get near them, down came a shower of bursts all round him, and it was a positive miracle that no one was hurt. My dog, who must be in at everything and jumped across to a machine gun, was the only casualty; he got a slight flesh wound in the back. We could do nothing but look on.

The bombers unloaded their eggs. They hummed about our ears and sent dirt and stones flying up all over the place. But they did little damage; they all fell out of harm's way, except one that came down on an uninhabited house and laid it in ruins.

But the scouts were most effective. One of Jagdstaffel 23's

hangars went up in flames and burnt to the ground with seven machines inside it. The bullets rattled like hail on the roofs.

The English were most amazingly impertinent and hardly knew how to find outlets for their arrogance. We had a huge notice-board at the entrance to the aerodrome—about seven metres long and two metres high—which warned other troops that they were forbidden to enter. One of the fellows up above hit on the idea of knocking it over, and pounded away at its thick wooden posts until his bullets cut right through them.

We could only look on and take care to show as little of ourselves as possible. Our only hope was that a neighbouring Staffel to which we had telephoned for help, would come in time.

But the storm vanished as quickly as it came. Up went a Verey light as the signal; off went all the machines and vanished in the west.

Then it was up to us to salvage what could be salvaged. There were smoking, burning masses all around us, and all our squads were busy with the extinguishers. The burning hangars collapsed; we could do no more in that direction, but we succeeded in fighting the fire down and preventing it from spreading to other buildings.

The damage was considerable. Strangely and luckily we had no casualties. A tent and two big sheds were burnt down. Eleven machines were total write-offs, and all the others except three were badly damaged.

It was a big score for the English, because they managed to put a whole Staffel out of action for several days by one fell swoop. Even if we suffered only material damage, it hit us very hard in view of the difficulties in getting replacements. All the same we had the pleasure of knowing that we had to lament the loss of no human lives and the consolation that the only machines destroyed were the old ones. It meant that we would have to get our new Fokkers all the earlier.

But when we cleared up the mess we discovered another loss. Under the ruins of the house hit by the bomb we found the two horses. As they were stabled in the building, the bomb killed them.

And so our gallant steeds were permitted to die a hero's death.

Chapter *VI*
ON LEAVE

S o we are unable to fly. Several days are bound to elapse before
our damaged machines can be repaired and replacements arrive
for those we have lost. Having nothing of importance to do, I
decide to utilise the brief leisure by going home on leave.

Suddenly a vision rises up in my soul, a gay, fair vision. It shows
me a land where there are no shell-holes, no ruined houses, no mass
graves . . . a land wherein peace dwells. It will be so still in this land;
no propeller will hum in its skies, and there will be no permanent
wall of gunfire on its western borders.

I will go to seek this land.

The wheels roll, Cambrai disappears.

The Belgian countryside flits past the windows; it is quite di-
verting to look at, but it passes too slowly. I have to change in Brussels, where there is a couple of hours wait. Brussels was always such
a beautiful town, but to-day she has lost her charms, and so I remain close to the station so as not to miss the train. At last we are
off again.

Onward, onward. The way is infinitely long, but every time the
wheels knock, it means the end of a rail. Every new rail is a couple
of metres nearer home. I hear nothing but that knocking, while my

eyes take in the ever-changing picture of the landscape quite automatically.

Night comes, and day follows it.

At Cologne we cross the Rhine. Now home is not far. But the train is still a part of the front; it passes through the land of peace like an alien spectre.

The carriages are full to overflowing. Every seat is occupied, and the corridors are blocked with men, packs and packages.

Everywhere I see grave men in field-grey. Tired faces stare out at the passing fields; there is no pleasure written in them. The front is still reflected in every eye; the roar of the cannon sounds in all our ears.

Hardly a word is spoken. We must first acclimatise ourselves to the different life that is lived here.

Gradually the eyes open wider and assume a happier look. Like children's eyes that gaze upon a Christmas tree.

Slowly the front fades away. At every station the field-grey in the train diminishes. Civilian garments mingle with the uniforms.

The spell is broken; everyone is talking and laughing again. I listen to the others, but cannot understand what they are saying. They discuss a thousand different things . . . trivialities which they consider important. No one speaks of the war, battles or death.

I am alone among civilians, and the nearer the train takes me to my home, the more I feel that it is journeying to a foreign land.

Now the wheels glide over the points, and we swing into the big station. Munich!

I remember when I was a small boy and visited this city for the first time with my father. It was evening; rain had fallen. The lights shone bright, and were mirrored on the wet asphalte. The illuminated shop-windows, the rows of pearls formed by the lamps of the long streets and the crowds of people made me feel I was in fairyland. So it will be to-day, for we have become children once more!

But there are only a few people at the station.

The lights are dimmed. The arc lamps are covered with blue shades to prevent any rays rising up from them. Ah, Munich has been forced to don war-garb! Just because some French airman took it into his silly head to drop a couple of bombs there!

Poor Munich, there was no need for you to shed your radiance. Anyone can see you from afar.

The fairy town has lost its magic.

I enter a restaurant near the station for a bite of something and promptly meet a good old friend.

"Hello, where do you come from? Still alive? So they've not shot you down yet?"

"No, not yet—as you see. I've only got a couple of days leave. It's not so easy out there, with the enemy outnumbering us. But we'll manage the business all right."

Oh, stop talking about the war. We're fed up with the beastly swindle. I'm earning quite a decent bit on army contracts, but food costs such a lot. If you want a decent meal, you've got to get the stuff by backstair ways, and that swallows up huge sums. Yes, things are in a terrible way with us. You fellows out there have a good time; you get enough to eat and drink; you've a jolly life and no worries."

I take refuge in silence. What could I tell him? The man has become a complete stranger to me; there is a deep gulf between us. We have nothing more to say to one another.

I am glad that my train is going on soon, so that I have an excuse to leave him.

Home to my father in Starnberg!

It is deep night now. I stand before our house.

One window is lighted. My father sits in that room, waiting for me. My hand feels for the name-plate on the door. Then the bell peals shrilly.

Lights blaze up in the house. I hear steps coming down the

stairs; father's slippers shuffle across the tiles of the passage.

Slowly the door opens. At last I am home again.

We sit opposite one another across the wide table. I gaze at father's high forehead and the hair that has grown grey now. I stroke the hands that are always busy on some work of art and have now grown so thin. For a long time we sit in silence.

"And so you're here again?"

"Yes."

"And you've kept well."

"Yes."

There were so many things I wanted to tell him, and now every word is so difficult.

War maps hang on the walls; the front lines are drawn on them. My letters lie neatly arranged on the table.

This is a gentle reproach to me for not having written more often. But what good would it do him to get a letter from me every day? Every one of them would take a few days to reach him, and anything could happen in the interval.

Anything could happen.—But this 'anything' means only one thing. My father has no one but me.

I ask whether there is a great shortage of food.

"Oh, no. We get enough to eat. And we invent all sorts of things so as to vary the menu. Dandelion soup, and nettles for spinach. We don't mind going hungry a bit as long as you people at the front get your meals. What do our little worries matter in comparison to the risks you are always taking?"

A silent night. I lie in bed in my old room and stare at the silhouettes of the furniture which I have seen all my life before the war; I hardly recognise it now.

Cool night air comes in through the open window; outside the stars hang peacefully in a black velvet sky. None of them move, none of them fade out; no new ones flame up.

There is a deep silence all round me. It is oppressive. My ears listen again and again for the noises; my eyes seek the shell-bursts. But everything around me remains quiet and peaceful.

Everything here has become alien to me. I do not fit in with these peaceful surroundings. My uniform lies on a chair where it does not belong, my boots on a carpet that is not accustomed to them.

There is no peace yet, but only war. And the war calls to me. Even in this first night the voice of the war warns me and shows me the way back.

The next day I meet a friend. He was in the field artillery, but was wounded and so came home. With him I shall be able to pass a few pleasant hours.

His wounds are healed; he can return to the front soon. "When are you going back?" I ask, "and where's your unit now?"

"I've no intention of going back; I'm not quite mad. My wound is one that just enables me to dodge further active service. I shall put in a bit of time with the depot, and then go my own way. You'd better stop at home too. It's all no use out there."

For a long time I pondered over those words.

Who is right? So many people speak in this strain, and so few think differently. Shall I stay at home too? No, even if I wanted to, I could not do it. The front calls me, my Staffel needs me; I am at home out there.

How many changes are taking place! What changes are going on in men's natures! Again I have lost a friend.

My boat floats on the waves. Nature has remained her old self. The lake rocks me as a mother rocks her child in soft, kind arms. The mountain range to southward is veiled in a light haze, but the sun carves a broad flaming pathway across the water; flies dance in it, and gulls and swallows dart hither and thither in the air. The reeds rustle along the boats edge and chirp like crickets in the wind.

My beautiful country!

A steamer moors at the landing stage. Young lads and their sweethearts alight. They bawl and swear, many reel drunkenly; one throws a wine-bottle across the gangway.

Young lads who earn huge sums of money by working in the munition factories, while their fathers suffer and die at the front. There is so much rottenness in the country, so much injustice. For what are we fighting then? For the fatherland? Or perhaps, to protect a beautiful country?

The war has become a business. A business with retail trading and wholesale profiteering. Men make money in the war through the war. A stock exchange report is more important than a casualty list.

What a lottle of troubles there are here! Of course there is a firing line somewhere; well, maybe . . .

How many reported killed? thirty thousand? Well, maybe— but the hundredweight of potatoes has gone up in price again, and a pound of flour costs a couple of pfennigs more.

That is our fatherland!

We stand so alone. For what do we go on fighting? We take no part in politics; we have no notion what is discussed and decided in the councils of the great.

We go on fighting, because it is our duty to do so. Because we still have a feeling of decency left in our bodies, because we can not drop a business we began. We must go on fighting, because we know of nothing else and can do nothing else.

War has become eternal in us.

Yet there is one being who will understand me.

A woman.

There is something else for which we can fight. We are still young; we have ideals and need a star to guide us on our way. To-morrow I shall go back to the front, but all to-day shall belong to this woman.

When the field-post came and brought me a letter in the familiar handwriting, I knew that the day was really beautiful. On the notepaper there was still a faint perfume where her hand rested, and the written lines spoke of her love. I always wore a locket that contained a lock of blonde hair—it was my talisman.

There were often flowers in her letters. I knew that it was spring when a primrose or violet lay between her sheets. I thought of our walks amid the young green of the beech-trees.

I saw rose leaves on her written lines and knew that it was summer. I remembered how we lay together in a boat, in a silent bay where weeping willows shielded us from the sun's fiercest rays. When the scent of the water was in the air, telling us of the joy of bathing.

Asters came, and it was autumn. And the foliage grew as blonde as your hair, and the linden leaves fluttered down on to us like golden hearts. I gathered armfuls of their splendour and made you a bed of pure gold.

A fir-twig brought me winter. Once we went up into the mountains when the snow-flakes were falling. We were snowed up in a lonely hut. The frost groaned in the trees outside, and the wind heaped millions of crystals about our shelter. But inside we were so snug and warm; the fire told us tales as it crackled, and the flames quivered with joy when their gleam met your eyes.

And once again it was spring with primroses and violets, and yet again it was summer with roses.

And now I am with you once more, and can take you in my arms again, you, my only woman.

"You—you—at last I have you again, and now I shall not let you go again. You must stay with me always."

"Yes, all to-day I shall be with you, the whole day and the whole night, but tomorrow I must go away again, back to the front."

"No, no, you mustn't. You must, must stay at home. Do what so many others have done. You can get yourself transferred to the depot; say your heart is affected—or something of the sort. Don't go back there again."

"But I can't do that. I must go back; I can't leave my Staffel in the lurch. Don't you understand that?"

Oh, never mind that stupid Staffel! You mustn't think of anything else but me."

In a cosy corner there stands a table, heaped with good things and delicious dainties. A little lamp illumines it with bright rays, leaving the rest of the room in semi-darkness. I recline on soft cushions and let myself be petted. I feel the presence of my beloved, and yet must keep a firm hold over my thoughts that always strive to wander afar.

We clink our glasses; the champagne pearls bubble in them. "Look at the pearls, beloved—they are like the tracer bullets when they shoot through the air from my machine-gun."

Ah, why must I always be thinking of the war? I sit here, gorging myself, and ought to be happy, and away over yonder the front is roaring. I cannot stay here any longer. I cannot do what the others have done. Not even for your sake. Do understand that; you must understand it—you—you above all people.

It grows cold in the room. There is no pressure from the hand that lies in mine when I say farewell.

Home melts away into a cold night. The last emotion has fallen from me like a warm cloak. I comprehend nothing more and have but a single longing—back to the front.

Goodbye, father, you are all that remains to me. You are my childhood, my genesis; you are my island in the alien sea. If only I could take you with me.

Away, away!

The train starts. My leave is behind me.

So many thoughts are dead. Behind me lies a mass grave. Rottenness and injustice—I will not think of it, I will not brood over it, I should gain nothing thereby.

The train carries me onward—away, away!

Somewhere on my journey there are woods and hills, somewhere there is a river which is called the Rhine. Many towns pass by me, many lights. Deep night.

At last the train pulls up in Cambrai. A car from my Staffel is waiting at the station; two comrades have come to meet me. Now I am at home again.

The rough cobblestones jolt and shake the car. A siren screams out. A warning against enemy aircraft. Archies begin to bark. The streets empty themselves. Somewhere a bomb crashes down.

But I sit in the car with a radiant face and feel that I have nothing more to desire. My companions summon me to tell them about my leave.

"It was good to be on leave—but the return was better. And the best of all is the homecoming to the Staffel!"

Chapter *VII*
THE ENGLISH OFFENSIVE

8.8.18. A misty morning, followed by a bright day. We are lying by our machines, having received orders to stand by. It is very quiet at the front, uncannily quiet.

We do not feel at ease in the sunshine. There is something brewing in the air. We are conscious of a depression, but do not know its cause.

We pass the time away with all sorts of useless things. We take a series of groups with the cameras because we are all nicely together. I telephone to other Staffels and try to find out what is the trouble, but no one knows anything. Then I go to the telescope and search the heavens. No aircraft to be seen, no shell-bursts from the Archies, not even a captive balloon. Above us there is a clear blue sky; its only inmates are a few swallows that dart hither and thither as though the air belonged to them to-day. My dog, Wart, frisks about the aerodrome, tries to dig out field-nice and wags his tail as he wipes his earthy nose on my breeches.

An artillery waggon rumbles along the road to Cambrai. Then all is quiet once more.

Far away from the south comes a low thud, with a rattling here and there. It is nothing. Quite likely it is the ammunition waggon jolting over cobble-stones.

Our ears strive to catch signs of life—firing or the drone of engines. But they find only an empty silence.

At last the order to start arrives. We are to escort a reconnaissance machine, which we shall find flying at three thousand metres over a certain locality at a certain time.

We swim our machines up into the blue summer air and circle over the meeting-place. It is not long before the blue fuselage of a Hannoveraner climbs up to us; I fly close to this two-seater and greet its occupants. The observers signs to me that he wants to climb higher before we cross the lines. I therefore hang on behind and down a bit and climb slowly upward, with the Hannoveraner always a bit before and below us.

Slowly the countryside recedes to eastward. The villages diminish in sizes, the rivers are only tiny, dainty lines on the earth's surface.

The brown ribbon of the front-lines draws nearer. I scan the heavens. No enemy aircraft to be seen. Only a very few shells bursting round the trenches.

But there is a thick haze to southward. In some parts it hangs close to the ground, like a yellow fog. I locate it as somewhere round about the Roman road, close to Amiens.

Can an attack be taking place in that direction? Am I looking at cascades of dust thrown up by drum fire, by bursting shells? Or is it only the ordinary haze we always find to southward on sunny days?

And why should there be anything particular happening today? It is so quiet everywhere. But it is the quietness—yes, just this quietness that is so uncanny.

We are now five thousand metres up. I see the observer of the Hannoveraner motioning us forward; he wants to get to work now. I wave back to him, and off we go. We climb a bit higher, close up our formation and hang on behind the two-seater.

The first puffs of white cottonwool make their appearance in the air and pass away under our wings. More and more of them come up, but they are a good five hundred metres below us. Now a couple of them rise up to our height and hover quite near to us. One hears something like a faint smack when they burst close to a machine, but we are used to them and do not let them worry us.

I search the heavens and then scan every fold in the ground— no aircraft about. Ever and again I look up into the sun, where the greatest danger lurks, whence sooner or later an enemy must make his appearance. Nothing!

The observer in the machine in front is photographing. He indicates his objectives to his escort and flies round them in wide circles. We hang on to him like a gaudy tail, flying wherever he flies. My ear listens to the roar of the engine; my eyes read the rev-counter, oil gauge, petrol clock. Everything in order. Then I count my flock. All there. We carry on with the flying.

The shell-clouds are now very thick. A mighty discharge from many batteries bursts at five hundred metres below us. We begin a series of erratic turns and zigzags—a trick!

A very old trick, but one that is good enough to catch the gunners down below and lead them to imagine that their bursts are sitting so near as to worry us. They blaze away with all the stuff they can get out of their barrels, hanging their white draperies on an invisible clothes-line well below us, while we rejoice in our safety.

The enemy aerodromes are below us, but they give no signs of life. What's up down there? The aerodromes are empty, but there are no enemy machines in the air. That means they must be busy somewhere else. Somewhere away to southward, perhaps—in the yellow haze. Are they taking part in an offensive?

The observer motions us homeward. A turn—noses eastward—push the stick down a bit to gain speed. Our job here is finished. I search the heavens and comb out the earth—but not a sign of an enemy. In the sun? No, nothing! Not one captive balloon up. The ground below us seems dead.

Archie's clouds diminish, but increase again as we cross the lines. At last a shell bursts in our midst. A couple of bullets rattle through my wings, but that is all. I count the machines; all there. Sergeant Schmidt sends a chuckle of pleasure across to me.

Nice fellow Schmidt. It does you good to know that there is a man just behind you who follows your trail like a bloodhound, who never swerves from it, but sticks in his place no matter how thick the shell-bursts may be or how wild the turns in a dogfight. I only need to bend my head slightly to the left to see his face, which is never without its friendly, cheerful grin.

Close behind me, but a bit above my head flies Schneider. An able, wary pilot, but one whose head is full of ideas that do not always work out so well. He would like to fight the war out all alone; he enjoys air duels and shooting up machine-gun nests.

When I turn my head to the right, I see another machine quite close to me. This is flown by Sergeant Prey, a serious fellow, who never laughs. But he never budges from his position, and nothing that happens in the air escapes his eye. But to-day even he is laughing with glee because we got away with it so nicely.

The observer fires a light-signal. We are dismissed. I fly close up to him and give him a parting handwave. He drops down and flies homeward.

We turn round again towards the front to see whether there is any change down below. It is as quiet as ever. No machines to be seen far and wide, except two German ones flying at low heights. A few shells bursting near the trenches. But otherwise nothing unusual.

The haze to southward grows thicker. I should have liked to fly over there and see what it meant. But petrol is running out, and so we must go home.

We hardly landed before I was called to the telephone. There

I obtained reliable information about the haze in the south; it was an English offensive on a large scale, launched south of the Somme on both sides of the Roman road. We were told to stand by for further orders.

Once again we lay beside our machines on the aerodrome, waiting for the telephone message that might come any minute to order us southward. But no message came.

We waited and waited. All around us was a silence of the grave.

Those were bad hours for us; we knew that a fierce battle was in progress to southward and could easily imagine the trouble the enemy's great numerical superiority in aircraft would cause. We knew how few Staffels were available for defensive purposes, even when all those belonging to the adjacent army corps were utilised. And yet we sat here tight, and no one summoned us. I got on the telephone to the officer commanding the flying groups in our army corps and asked for his permission to take off. No, we were to stand by for further orders, he replied.

A terrible suspense.

Towards evening we were sent up again. Not to the south; we merely escorted another reconnaissance machine. The result was a short flight in our own sector, with a couple of fights, but nothing particular happened.

The haze still hung to southward. It grew, and spread eastward. In the darkness of evening the fire blazed from the mouths of countless guns.

Night falls on our aerodrome. We know now what is happening. Flames flash and quiver on the horizon; we also hear the roll of the guns and can even distinguish some particularly violent explosion. Is this due to the south-east wind that carries the echo to us, or has the front changed—has it come nearer to us? Or is it merely the night that magnifies every sound? tomorrow we shall know for certain; tomorrow they will throw us into the fighting down there.

At 11 p.m. the telephone rattles again. The Staffel is ordered to hand over every available lorry for troop transports. Ah-ha, now the gentlemen of the staff are beginning to bestir themselves. Well, as long as they have reserves to throw into the line, all right.

We have four serviceable lorries available. Take plenty of spares along with them, you drivers, for who knows when and in what condition we shall see them again. There's thick air at the front.

The lorries rattle away. The houses throw the echo back to us; then all is silence again, save for an occasional vehicle on the high road, which the night soon swallows up.

I cannot rest. I wander along the aerodrome, sit down on the edge of a ditch and stare out into the night.

The roll of the guns grows ever louder to southward.

Now the rattle of wheels and the rumble of engines reaches me more frequently from the road. More and more lorries, hastening southward, bringing up reserves to the threatened front. Daylight will soon be at hand; then we can fly and shall know for certain what it all means.

9.8.18. The telephone rattles away in the early hours of the morning. Urgent orders to stand by. The order to take off will come soon. The English attack down there is continuing. Our people have been forced back a fair distance. The actual front line is not yet clear. We must fly cautiously, as there are strong enemy forces in the air. Can we spare any more lorries for troop transports? No. We must keep a sharp look out at the aerodrome, because further air raids by the English are probable.

RRRRRRR . . . Telephone. Rrrrrrr . . . telephone again . . . questions, orders . . . And so it goes on for some little time.

At last the order to start. We are to go southward.

We are flying towards the front. Five machines. We cannot raise more. A great pity; we could do with them to-day. If only we had the Fokkers! But it's all the same now.

The weather has turned bad; it is thick and cloudy. Our visibility is very poor.

We are flying from the north, past Bapaume, Courcelette and Albert, between the Ancre and the straight road that leads to Amiens. The hell is on our left.

We cannot see much of the ground now. Nothing but smoke and haze—natural and artificial fog mingle. The air seethes and quivers with the explosions.

Aircraft at all heights. Single machines and thick swarms. We shall find foemen everywhere to-day.

We are flying low, at one thousand metres.

There are fights in the upper air; there are fights in the lower air. The numerical superiority of the enemy gives him the advantage. So it does not matter where we fight. But down below we can keep the enemy a bit away from our infantry. So down we go.

Now we are in the thick of it. We are attacked at once by scouts. Turns—shooting—carry on! One, two, three, four machines behind me; we are still together. Carry on!

The machines dance and rock in the eddies set up by the shells. The Somme flows below us. A village—Corbie, maybe—carry on!

Air fights. More scouts attack us. Turn—shoot—turn. One, two, three, four machines behind me. Good; carry on! The Roman road, Villers Bretonneux. Where is the front?

Few explosions here. The smoke is on our left. On the roads thick columns of infantry, lorries, batteries, all in khaki uniforms. English—lay in to them with the machine-guns! Then carry on eastwards—along the road!

An English formation advances towards us: ten, twenty, thirty machines, scouts and two-seaters. They fly past us at fifty metres distance and just a bit above us. Their cockades look almost near enough to touch. But they fly past without attempting to go for us. Either they did not recognise us, or did not want to.

Carry on!

Where is the front?

Guns firing below us, here, there, everywhere. All khaki uniforms. Englishmen.

Two-seaters in front of us, between us, behind us. Turn, shoot, carry on!

Crash! A couple of shell-splinters from below pass through my wings. Carry on!

Crash, crash! Earsplitting detonations. My machine slips from one side to the other, shoots up, is pulled down again. One, two, three, four machines behind me; carry on!

Where is the front?

No more columns below, but the ground swarms with men in brown. They crouch in every shell-hole and run forward along every hollow. Grey, squat things roll through their midst—tanks. Here, there, everywhere. Carry on!

Left-hand turn. The wooded patches at Cerisy whirl past me. I know them so well from of old.

The Somme valley again. Steep slopes, lakes, water. No field grey troops here either. Carry on!

A scrap with two-seaters. The dogfight sways westward, past Hamel and Hamelet. We are over Corbie again. Turning and shooting. I am sitting on one of them. Three others sitting on me. The machine in front of me smokes and sideslips, takes fire, drops down somewhere. Incendiary bullets whistle round my head. Turn—carry on!

Scouts fly up from the right, blue-grey, Germans. Fokkers. The dogfight grows bigger and bigger.

Back to eastward. One, two, three machines behind me, where's the fourth? There it is, coming over from the left. Thank heaven, we are still all together. Carry on!

Hamel, Cerisy, Morcourt. Brown troops, brown troops, no grey. Where is the front?

A Staffel approaches us; Fokkers; silver tails, coloured stripes on the fuselages. Hurrah, the 34th! My old Staffel. The machine with the two red stripes. Hurrah, Greim! A brief wave to him; carry on!

English machines, double-seaters, scouts. Turn, shoot, carry on!

Everything roars and seethes below us and around us. Froyart. Still no grey troops. Where is the front?

Foucaucourt lies below me; my old aerodrome, dead and empty. Shells burst on it, tearing up the surface that we were at such pains to level. Small holes, huge craters. The place is just as we found it in the spring. The scars caused by the Battle of the Somme have broken out again; the land is bleeding from a thousand wounds.

At last grey soldiers. Sparsely spread out; here a machine-gun nest, there a field-gun.

Turn, turn back. Here is a big brown patch behind a tank—English infantry—at them with the machine-gun. See them scatter—carry on!

Fight with scouts. Turn—shoot—carry on!

My petrol clock's hand is getting suspiciously near zero. We must go back. Turn—homewards.

One, two, three, four machines behind me. We have all come through safe and sound. We drop down to our aerodrome on the last drops of petrol from our emergency tanks.

So the enemy has started his great offensive.

With a huge expenditure of men and materials he has overrun our positions on the Roman road and advanced a considerable distance. He very nearly managed to break through.

We suffered severe losses, especially in prisoners. Were our troops overwhelmed, or is their spirit no longer the old one? Has it degenerated?

Our people are worried about the future. We have learnt very little about the situation. Every morning we get a report on the position of the front lines—as far as the staff know it—and in the evening we get the official communiqué. That is all; if we want to know anything more, we must find it out over the telephone or go and look for ourselves. Moreover we really do not need to know much; we just fly and fight in the way we are used to. No official communiqué can alter our mode of life. The three Staffels comprising our group work in an alternation that never varies. Two hours flying, two hours rest or free hunting, two hours to stand by. And so it goes on from dawn to dusk. Between times we have a few special missions such as escort duty, contact patrols when our infantry are attacking and mass flights in squadron formation when the air is thick with enemy machines.

We do not ask what else is happening in the world; we simply do our duty and fly. We have a world of our own, which is so large and beautiful that we need no other.

10.8.18. The enemy has split his aerial forces up again. We meet Englishmen flying over Arras at all heights, but they are not in a particularly aggressive mood to-day.

The battle area south of the Somme is still thick with ground fighting formations and artillery spotters, but there are not so many scouts about.

Not so many shells are bursting down below now. The road between Villers Bretonneux and Harbonnières is still under heavy fire. The bursts there must come from German cannon because this district is in enemy occupation. Perhaps a counter-attack? We do not know.

The clouds hang thick at one thousand metres. Yesterday's bad weather is breaking and dissolving into white balls of cloud. The clouds divide the fighting into two halves; the two-seaters— ground fighters and escorts—are battling with one another down below, while up above the scouts are scrapping on their own. We have enough to do in the upper regions, and so find it necessary to drop down. To-day our best plan is to keep the enemy scouts away from our working machines. And so we fly and fight.

18.8.18. Things are beginning to move in our Arras sector too. Gommécourt and Tilloy were under heavy fire as far back as the 14th. On the 16th the whole front from Arras to the Somme and even further southward was ablaze. The smoke trails extend unbroken until they merge into the horizon. Probably there is firing going on right down to Soissons. We cannot worry our heads much about the neighbouring sector as we have far too much work to do in our own, and too few arms and eyes to do it.

The weather looks like changing. Visibility is very clear, though somewhat impeded by clouds. Many English captive balloons are in the air; we can see the taut, yellow shimmer of their thick bags across the void.

The fire is heaviest between Boiry and Courcelles. Far below a Staffel of German fighters is flying to the trenches from northward. A large English scout squadron is about to dive on these machines, but we arrive in the nick of time to take the enemy in the flank. The odds are against us, but our attack affords some relief to the fighting Staffel down below.

We are turning and shooting again. An upward and downward surging of machines. I have hardly time to give a fleeting glance to our direction every now and then. Tracer lines hang in the air like spiders' webs. More blue-green machines come along; another German Staffel attacks the enemy. The fight is more even now, but we are still in the minority. Then the English machines detach themselves from the melée and make off westwards.

There is a gap in the machines behind me.

Where is Schneider?

He is not up above. I search the sky, but there is no sign of him. Deep below me are the fighters, still circling over the trenches. What's over there by the wooded patches? Two artillery fliers. Not a trace of our machine anywhere.

Has Schneider been shot down? I fly over the area of our recent battle and drop down, scanning every metre of ground below, but find nothing. He is not above me, he is not in the air at all, but he must be somewhere.

Down yonder, at the very edge of the trenches, there lies a fuselage and a couple of broken wings. Is that his machine? No, it is an English one that was shot down a few days ago.

Where is Schneider? Perhaps he got a hit which forced him to pull out of the fight and go home. Perhaps one of the others knows something about him.

Home!

The flight-sergeant comes up to me. "Has Schneider landed?" I ask. "No, sir."

One machine after the other hovers over the aerodrome, lands and taxies to the hangars.

"Schmidt, have you seen anything of Schneider?"

"No."

"And you?"

"No."

"Do you know anything about Schneider?"

"No; he flew with us all the time; he was with us when we fought the scouts. I saw him when the other Staffel came along. Perhaps he hung on to them and went on flying."

"Perhaps."

But then he would be bound to come back soon because his petrol would run out. It is 5.20 now; he would have to land at 5.50 at the very latest.

Where can he be? I do not believe he flew along with the others. He is too experienced to mistake their machines for ours. But he is certainly not down anywhere.

No use telephoning yet; we can only wait. I sit down at the telescope and search the sky, but see nothing but blue air.

A machine looms up in the distance and approaches. That will be Schneider!

No. It is a two-seater that flies past us and disappears.

5.45. Not yet back. The neighbouring Staffel returns from the front and lands. None of our machines are with it.

He will not come now. Perhaps he made a forced landing somewhere.

I call up the front. The officer in charge of ground observation has seen us; he saw the whole of the fight. An English machine was forced down and just managed to land behind its own lines.

"An English machine? Quite sure it wasn't a German? One of ours is missing."

"No. I'm quite sure it was English. A Sopwith."

An artillery observer tells a similar tale. He too followed the fight from the ground and saw an English machine land.

"Was it really an Englishman?" I ask. "One of ours is missing." "Certainly it was English. We saw the cockades quite clearly and destroyed the machine by artillery fire."

Where can Schneider have got to?

Then Schmidt reports himself and stand before me in an attitude of embarrassment. "Perhaps I might know something about Schneider, sir," he volunteers.

"Well, what then? Did you see him?"

"No, but when the other Staffel joined in, he flew away—a long distance—and I believe he went across to attack a captive balloon."

"You're dotty. It'd be sheer madness!"

"Yes, sir, but Schneider often told me he was keen on getting a balloon and wanted to have a go at one at the first opportunity."

Yes, that will be the explanation. Those balloons were wonderfully clear. The dogfight was dying down. "I'll use the chance," he thought, and went off on the little trip. Not a bad idea in itself, but a criminal piece of carelessness, because there was a chain of scouts in the air to protect the balloons, and he was bound to see them.

There are two possibilities. If he has made a forced landing anywhere behind our lines, we shall get news of him. Then again he may have landed on some other aerodrome, where he will get petrol and fly home.

Slowly the evening falls. A summer evening is endlessly long. The sun goes down; long shadows stretch across the aerodrome.

Now they have disappeared; the sky is pale grey, with a blood-red ribbon across the western horizon. It is useless to go on searching the heavens with a telescope, because the dusk is on us and the twilight flickers in my eyes. Perhaps he may yet come. I order a huge flare in the aerodrome and tell the men to have the landing-lights ready.

Now the darkness falls apace. Cannot the day bide with us a bit—just another hour? Summer evenings are so short.

Our hopes fade away with the daylight.

Now the flare gleams more brightly than the sunset. The first range-finding shots of the machine-gun Archies ascends like stars to heaven. He has just enough light to land by.

But our bodies throw long shadows when we pass the flare. Night has descended on us.

An engine drones somewhere in the distance. Can that be he?

The flame receives a bucketful of petrol and shoots up on high. Sparks whirl and dance. I close my dazzled eyes; only my ears are attentive.

The drone grows stronger and then dies down. That was not Schneider. He will never come back.

We fire a couple of star-shells to give him the direction of the aerodrome. We know that it is in vain, but our hopes are born anew each time we watch the fiery tail sweep through the sky, listen to the bang and gaze at the sheaf of bright white stars. But as these stars die out, one by one, our hopes die with them.

Night and silence have descended on the aerodrome. The fire

has fallen on its ashes; once it quivered up faintly, and then this last light died away.

The sheds are shut, the tents are closed. They wait for no more aeroplanes.

He will not come. No telephone has called us, no report has come to hand.

No news came in the night, and none in the morning.

Nothing.

He will never return.

21.8.18. A day of heavy fighting on the ground and in the air. A glorious day, with a cloudless blue sky. From earliest dawn the air has hummed as though invaded by thousands of swarms of bees utilising the summer weather to gather in their food. But who has a thought for bees and summer to-day?

With the first rays of light we start off on escort duty for contact patrols. Back again, fill up with petrol, then off to the front again: barrage patrol and protection for captive balloons.

Flying activity is now at its height. All the sky is dotted with floating points. There is so much room in the air for them, but unfortunately most of them are English. To-day we have no time to look what is going on below; the foeman of the air claims our undivided attention. We know the approximate course of the front line and are not interested in anything else.

We are over the lines and proceed to chase away a couple of English machines that are spotting for their artillery. An English formation approaches from the west; the machines look huge, but are apparently single-seaters. A new type we have not seen before. They must be the new Sopwith Dolphins, about whose speed and climbing capacities we have heard such wonderful tales. Once more it is our fate to run up against a new type of English machine while swimming along in our old boats!

But what's the good of swearing! It is just a fact that the other side is better off in all respects, and we have long been accustomed to flying about as targets in the air, even if it is not exactly a pleasant business.

Flying somewhat higher, the Sopwiths dive down to attack us. We fly round in a narrow circle for mutual protection. Now they are coming down, one after the other. Each sparks out a couple of shots at us, then pulls his stick, shoots up over our heads and vanishes into the stately heights. Not very dashing tactics, but we have no objection.

So it goes on for a while; then the English make off in a southwesterly direction. In the north a couple of double-seaters pop up to spot for their artillery or pursue some other noble purpose. This time we can play the big bad bully and assault them, but they see us in time and fly far away into their hinterland. Archies bark at us in their efforts to demonstrate that there are still some people on the ground who take an interest in us. We must take care not to drift too far behind the enemy's lines to-day, because there is a strong east-wind propelling us in that direction.

Despite the many machines in the air to-day there is not much doing in the fighting way. Everyone seems to be very keenly on the alert against surprises. So we fly our patrol and protect the balloons; luckily no enemy aircraft make any serious attempt to interfere with them. We are relieved by the neighbouring Staffel, whereupon we fly home and land.

Our aerodrome was hardly recognisable. It positively swarmed with machines on the ground—all Fokkers. Jagdgeschwader No 1 had landed on our place, and is to work on the front area occupied by the 17th Army Corps.

That was a pleasure. A strong reinforcement for us. Our battle ardour received an impetus at once. God fights on the side of the stronger battalions.

We greet old friends and admire the many beautiful Fokkers— not without a certain envy.

Telephones rattle. The squadron takes off. We receive urgent orders to stand by. The drone of engines in the air makes a glorious melody; now we can rejoice wholeheartedly in the fine summer's day.

Archie's cloudlets mount into the blue sky. English bombing squadrons are on their way. Naturally they have their own devices for utilising the glorious weather, just as we have. The telephone rattles again; we are to take off in squadron formation.

All the three Staffels together. I am to lead them. What more can I want today?

Off! I head the formation with seven machines. Staffel 23 has nine serviceable machines and flies on my left, while the seven of the 32nd are on my right. Twenty-three machines, and all German.

What a splendid picture all these glittering machines behind me make! They seem to be standing still in mid air; the only sign of motion I can see is a slight swaying up and down. They are peaceful ships on a huge ocean.

The activity at the front has increased. Machines are positively swarming there.

Suddenly I see flashes from circling wings; Jagdgeschwader 1 is fighting over yonder. We hasten to join in, but a large English formation comes up on our right and tries to get across. So it's up to us to block their way!

Squadron meets squadron. Our numbers are about even. Each man picks out an opponent and the turns begin. The result is a mad whirlpool.

Another English squadron joins in, and yet another. Round and round we go. I keep an eye open to see we do not drift too far over the lines.

A bright flame shoots out somewhere; then smoke begins to rise. A machine is burning—an English machine. One of ours goes down in a spin, then flies homeward. Badly hit, perhaps.

Jagdgeschwader 1 comes along from southward to join us. Now a real aerial battle is in progress.

An Englishman goes down in a spin and crashes. Another English machine takes fire and drifts through our midst in most eerie fashion. But when it has dropped about one thousand metres, it explodes and shivers into burning fragments.

The turns continue until I am almost giddy with them. Then the English machines gradually emerge from the dogfight and disappear into the western sky.

We rally and fly along the front for a while. There is not much to do; a couple of English machines that have been spotting for their artillery make off in good time and fly homewards.

A long tail of Archie's cloudlets marks our way. The gunners are in a furious temper and plaster the sky with their bursts. They get through large quantities of ammution, with no success.

To-day we drop home with feelings of pride. At least we have the superiority in the air once more!

Towards evening we take off again in squadron formation. The English retire as soon as we approach. We have only one brief encounter with a scout squadron, which makes off in a very short space of time. Below us our working machines can do their jobs in peace—there are also no English machines at the front to harass our infantry. To-day it is a pleasure to be a German pilot.

Once again night has fallen on the aerodrome; searchlights shine out and Archies begin to shoot. The fine weather and bright moon are driving the bombers out of their sheds.

That does not worry me. Having taken off so many times to-day, I can just as well try another flight at night. There is so much going on to-night; all over the dark sky I hear the drone of English machines. They want to make up for time lost during the daylight.

I have made all necessary arrangements and shall take off at 11.45 p.m.

Again I fly over a countryside wrapped in night and moonlight. Again I fly through the chill loneliness.

Shell bursts and searchlights wander towards me. A huge machine looms up before me—a gigantic shadow that flits across the moon. A cone of searchlights touches it, circles round it and then wanders onward with it.

I go into a turn and hang on behind the machine. My eyes are glued to the black silhouette; I am not going to lose that prize. Nearer and nearer I come; already I can distinguish the details. There are two engines in separate cockpits and the under wings are shorter than the upper ones. It must be a Handley Page.

I rejoice mightily, for such a big fat bird has never yet fallen to my guns.

Now I am quite near. The searchlight throws a livid gleam on the enemy's fuselage; I can see the forms of both pilot and observer. The sparks from the exhaust whirl through the air and hit me in the face.

My eye goes down behind the notch, my finger presses the trigger-button—just as the livid light flashes into my machine. I am blinded—caught by the searchlight, while a wall of blackness has risen up between the Englishman and me.

I fire off a series automatically in the direction of my target. Perhaps I may score a hit or two as we are so near. But the searchlight clings to me like an iron band I give the sign by throttling down three times, but the searchlight ignores it and sticks to me.

I put the machine into a sharp turn and swerve out of the light. My eyes are blind.

Where is the enemy?

No sign of him in the former direction; no machine up above or down below. I cut my engine and glide down slowly and softly. Perhaps the searchlight will get the Englishman again if it hears the drone of only one machine.

The cone of light dances and circles round the sky, but never comes to rest again anywhere for long. All in vain.

I open up my engine again so as not to lose too much height

and make a thorough search myself. Nothing to be seen anywhere. I wait up a bit longer, but to no purpose. The enemy has vanished and cannot be found.

I throw down a few juicy curses to those searchlight fellows, but that is all I can do. Oh, what asses! That Englishman would not have got away if the damned searchlight had not blinded me. But cursing is no good; though it relieves one's feelings, it does not make the air any warmer.

It is icy cold; tired of hanging about, I come down and land. Not a very good landing. Bump! then another bump—the axle is bent and the wheels look decidedly knockneed. That is the result of cursing too much and not looking out properly.

24.8.18. A glorious message has come through the telephone. Six Fokkers are waiting at the park for us to fetch them. Great rejoicing throughout the Staffel. Our six oldest machines are wheeled out for the exchange. An Albatros, two Pfalzs and three Rolands.

Now comes the burning question: who is to fly the new machines? Eight pilots and six machines; two must be disappointed. I decide that the two who were the last to join the Staffel must be the ones to wait. That is the fairest solution, especially as the two juniors have not had much experience of the front.

We others climb into the old bags of tricks, and take off. My engine can only manage eleven hundred revs, but no matter—it will hold out as far as the park.

We fly over peaceful villages and beautiful country. But we are not interested in the scenery to-day.

At last the park aerodrome looms up. We land and taxi to the sheds. Swiftly we switch off our engines and climb out of the old boxes. We don't care a damn what happens to them next.

Where are the Fokkers?

I report to the technical officer, who reels off a few numbers and presses a couple of documents into my hand. These make us the happy owners of six Fokkers, which are standing in a hangar. The mechanics make them ready and fill up. That takes time, and meanwhile we have a look round the park.

We see every possible type of machine in the hangars. Among the single-seaters there are a couple of new machines which are completely unknown to us . . . Fokker monoplanes with rotary engines. Wonderful things that look so light and nimble, Fokker's very latest invention. Jagdgeschwader 1 is to fly them, but for the present they must remain in the sheds because they are to be fitted up with a few improvements.

Good prospects for the future. Fokker is still the old Fokker, for every new machine he brings out is a considerable improvement on the last. Other firms also bring out new machines, but they are generally content with a few superficial alterations that do not effect much improvement in the flying and fighting capacities.

Our machines are ready. Everything is in order. I climb into my seat, which wears a somewhat unfamiliar aspect. I try the stick. Everything works easily.

The engine roars. The ground whirls away from under me. Swiftly we rise; the aerodrome and its hangars dwindle rapidly. The machines climb wonderfully and answer to the slightest movement of the controls. That will be a joy when we try our first fight in them. So now homeward, with all possible speed.

We land and put our treasures safely away in the hangars. The mechanics examine them thoroughly; the machine guns are loaded and tested. The painter marks them with the Staffel's badge, the arrowhead on the wings; then he paints the fuselages with the coloured bands that are the badges of the individual pilots. He takes particular pains with my machine, embellishing my lilac stripe with narrow black edges. Finally I tie the streamers that are the insignia of leadership to the end of the cockpit. Only then do the machines really belong to us.

We cannot go to the front to-day, but we practise our new birds instead. The more we get to know them, the better we are pleased with them. Whatever one tries—steeply banked turns, dives, loops—they always answer the controls beautifully; one catches the machine at once. They give one a magnificent feeling of safety.

Lieutenant Kämmerer wants to test his machine's climbing capacity to the utmost and makes an altitude flight. Just as he has reached some five thousand metres above Cambrai he sees a solitary English machine, a D.H.4 which appears to be photographing. Naturally he attacks it at once and swoops down on to it from behind. He presses the trigger-button, but not one shot leaves the barrel. The mechanic has given him no ammunition belts, because he wants to do something to the gun.

A painful predicament, but without ammunition it is impossible to shoot down any foeman. Yet, strangely enough, the Englishman goes down in steep spirals. Deeper and deeper, with Kämmerer close behind him all the time, until he makes a good landing near Bevillers. Kämmerer circles round proudly, but cannot prevent the crew from destroying their machine. That was the most harmless air-fight that ever took place, but it was a victory for Kämmerer all right.

Later we learnt from the prisoners that the observer's gun jammed after his first shot; as he could not get it right, he gave up the struggle. They were both blue with rage when we told them that their assailant had not a single shot in his gun.

Well, that sort of thing can happen. Unfortunately such bloodless battles are only exceptions.

It is snowing from a clear sky. Great white flakes are dancing down—leaflets.

No one knows where they come from. From a balloon or an aeroplane? The wind has carried them a long distance and sends them sailing through the air like white butterflies.

Our men run about the meadow like children, collecting these leaflets. It is quite a profitable business; they receive money for every leaflet they hand over and can earn quite decent sums on the large masses of them they often have to collect.

G.H.Q. prefers to buy them rather than have them left lying about to be read. But these measures are quite unnecessary; the leaflets would have done no harm in our ranks because even the stupidest soldier has seen through the trick and is therefore not to be influenced by such stuff. The men know quite well that the statements which are decked out as particularly pleasant truths contain the most lies.

The letters which Private X or Private Y write to their wives from prison camps, depicting the life there, with its concerts and theatrical performances—in the rosiest light, only make us smile. We also grin at the false reports of entente victories. And then the tales of reinforcements from America—so and so many thousand Americans embarked to-day and ever so many more are going off tomorrow—are nothing new to us. Every day we can see with our own eyes that the numbers on the other side are increasing and our own are diminishing.

No one worried about those leaflets formerly. We just did the right thing with them; the proper place for latrine tales is the latrine. It was very kind of the enemy to provide us with these luxuries, nice soft paper, which was generally printed on one side only.

But the value of these leaflets is greatly enhanced since the day that G.H.Q. first offered money for them. They became a sort of paper currency, subject to the same fluctuations as real banknotes. Now they are sought for eagerly, and the result is that the information they contain always gets read. But that does not matter particularly; in any case it is kind of the enemy to provide our men with a little extra money in this fashion.

Chapter *VIII*
CAMBRAI BECOMES
A BATTLE AREA

S TAFFEL affairs have given me much work lately. An order came for us to move back, and everyone has been busy packing up.

The front has come nearer to us. Every day we lose ground, here an odd corner, there a salient; it was not much at first, but afterwards large areas had to be evacuated to prevent certain sections being left unsupported. So it went on, and the result is that the enemy has gained a considerable stretch of ground. Bapaume and Combles have fallen; the line goes very close to Peronne.

Flights to the front became shorter and shorter; the artillery fire came nearer and nearer until shells from the heavy guns began to fall in villages quite near to us. So we had to clear out and beat a retreat.

At first we were given a new aerodrome at Erchin. But even this locality seemed too near, and we were therefore ordered to move to Lieu St. Amand.

The first transports have already gone off. One consignment after another is loaded up and despatched to the new haven of safety. This means much work, but for us it is only a minor business. The flying remains the chief consideration; on no account must our aerial activities suffer.

Heaven be praised, the enemy is not very active today. Nothing of note occurs on our patrols.

Tomorrow the removal will be finished. My trunks are packed; my pictures have come down from the walls; my books have disappeared. Deprived of its cloth, the table suddenly assumes a bare, forbidding aspect. The room in which I have lived so long has become quite a stranger to me.

The mess also looks bare. Only the scantiest necessities still remain. Pictures and lamps have been removed; the window frames stand out black in a livid light. The rooms have reverted to their former condition; they are plain, bare peasants' living quarters again.

I am most loath to depart, for I have learnt to love the village during my sojourn. The surrounding country was not a pretty landscape; the houses were insignificant red brick buildings. The fields were barren; the gardens could hardly muster a couple of trees. But we have grown used to the place.

Tomorrow all will be over.

We have become gipsies. We wander from place to place and have grown used to wandering. When we were with the troops we often changed our quarters daily, but now we take root for weeks and months. Yet the time comes at last when we have to resume our travels.

To-night we sleep here for the last time; tomorrow nothing that belongs to us will be here. Afterwards Epinoy will share the fate of so many other villages; shells will plough up the ground around it; a direct hit will land right in the middle of its houses, and then the fight will go on. It may be that the village will suffer little damage, it may be that it will be completely destroyed. From above we shall see it below us and think of it only as a village like so many others. It will have become a stranger to us. It will be relegated to the 'once upon a time.'

We are back from the front, and slowly the evening descends

upon us. That patrol was our last take off from here to the lines; tomorrow we shall land on the new aerodrome.

I fly off just once more, quite alone, to say farewell. Higher and higher I climb. The haze that extends to two thousand metres is left below me, as I soar up heavenwards in the pure sky of eventide.

My view is so clear and infinite to-day. When I reach five thousand metres, I can see the sea; it shines in the distance, glittering gold in the setting sun. I am looking on it for the last time.

We have never been able to reach it in our flights, and now a new strip of land is interposed between us and this distant water.

The villages have dwindled to tiny points; only the great highroads stretch wide and bright into the distance.

The front lines now run along by Roeux, Monchy, Vancourt and Croiselles. From my height I can no longer see the shell-bursts; the war has sunk to the depths, while around me all is peace and silence.

In the east there are small, round clouds, like celestial lambs grazing on the green pastures of heaven. Now all the edges are bordered with a red, through which they seem to gain in size.

Slowly these red fringes fade away. Now the clouds are blue-grey—merging into the general hue of the night.

The sun is a huge, blood-red ball, sinking into the sea.

From the depths its rays still gleam up heavenwards like the beams of a searchlight; then they too die down and follow the sun into the sea of infinity.

The air is thin in the great heights and lets the cold through to me. Or is it only the coming night?

It is a long way from the front to Arras now. Arras has almost become part of the base. The town lies directly beneath me, but I can only just recognise it. Mists rise up from the Scarpe and float over the town, wrapping all its buildings in a soft, blue veil. The only objects I can distinguish clearly are the jagged roadways of the citadel.

A solitary machine climbs up in my vicinity and approaches me. It is a single-seater, an English scout. At first we stare at one another across the void; then we attack and begin to turn. The turns grow narrower and narrower; nearer and nearer come our machines. I can see every detail of the other machine, the painted badges, the number, the bracing wires. Two red streamers float out from its elevator … the pilot is a streamer-man, like myself, a leader.

We meet alone in the great heights. What drives my opponent so late into this loneliness?

We still continue our narrow turns. Neither can get on the other's tail and put in a burst. I see his eyes peering out of his goggles and watch his hand on the stick.

Is it not senseless to think of fighting now?

The other pilot raises his hand and waves to me; simultaneously both machines pull out of their turns. Now they are flying side by side, quite close to one another—quite close.

Weary of the combat, two birds of prey soar through the evening sky on peaceful wings.

We have known one another a long time. Our formations have often met and fought at the front. Has peace come to the land now, so that we may fly tranquilly side by side?

We hold converse with one another; thereto we need no words; words would not help us here. We speak of the evening sky and the sun which has just set. We do not speak of the depths, of the ground far below us, and so we do not speak of the war. We speak of the air, of infinity, of eternity, of the stars.

Darkness grows around us. Only a faint gleam comes up to us from the lakes and rivers in the west that reflect the last brightness of the evening sky. Already it is quite dark in the east; the eye can see nothing more there when, dazzled by the western sky, it scans the depths.

I must go home.

The other pilot has a little more daylight, for he is flying in the direction of the sun. I wave to him for the last time; we detach our thoughts from one another and break off our flight. One machine goes into a wide turn and heads eastwards; the other flies to the west. The streamers swing out in opposite directions to give a farewell greeting.

The other machine vanishes into the evening sky, while I dive into the blue twilight.

Our thoughts turn back and sink earthward. The ground grows in size as it rises to meet me, and with it comes the war.

The evening star fades out in the haze. The lights below me are no longer an ocean that reflects eternity, but flashes from the cannon mouths and bursting shells.

My machine flits down to the aerodrome as the last rays of daylight fade out. I turn to the west and see that night reigns there too—deep night.

28.8.18. Our move is finished. The lorries have taken everything away. A fatigue party searches all the houses and sheds for anything that might have been left behind; then I hand over the quarters and aerodrome to the commandant of the village.

Hitherto our group have been its only occupants and undisputed rulers. But yesterday the infantry arrived, and a captain belonging to some divisional staff asserts his importance as village commandant. He wants us to furnish him with documents about the place and cannot understand that we don't give a damn for such things. I fancy, however, that he will not spend much time here as inkslinger in chief, because the English will soon come along and make short work of all his red tape.

We strike our tent-hangars, but the wooden sheds remain standing. We cannot take them along with us since time does not permit; moreover we do not need them as there are sheds to spare on the aerodrome to which we are moving. We receive instructions that we are not to destroy them, because they can serve as quarters for other troops.

Our aeroplanes stand on the meadow. The mechanics swing the propellers, and we are all ready to start. The last toolbags are stowed away on the last lorry, the water-buckets rattle as they are loaded up, the petrol hose is rolled up and disappears into the interior of the van. The works sergeant and a couple of mechanics stand by the lorry, waiting to see us take off before climbing in and driving away. Everything is ready. What are we waiting for?

A wagon column arrives on the aerodrome; the horses are unharnessed; the drivers stable their steeds in our sheds. There is much chatter and shouting; many 'whoas' and 'gee ups,' and a mighty rustle of straw.

The front has taken possession of our kingdom. Our rule is over.

Our engines are running smoothly. We taxi to the starting point. Once more I look back. That house was our mess, and that one my private quarters; there is the church tower with its four clocks and there are those other houses that were our billets.

A butterfly flits across the meadow towards me; he only just escapes the propeller. But he flutters sunnily onward, and I seem to be sitting on the grass, watching his flight. He jogs about all round my head until a slight breeze from the propeller catches him and whirls him away behind me. All over!

Off! The dry grass rustles for the last time as my wheels pass over it. Then the village dwindles into the distance below my wings until it finally vanishes from my sight.

Once upon a time—

It is easy to find the way to the new aerodrome. On our left is the Sensée canal, with all its lakes and marshes, a broad waterway visible from afar. Then the other canal from Cambrai looms up on our right, along with the Scheldt, which joins the Sensée canal at Étun. Finally we sight the point where three roads cross close to Bouchain, and just beside it lies Lieu St. Amand.

The aerodrome is a fine, big field, with a slight incline to eastward, but wonderfully smooth ground. No hollows or folds, and no ditches. An aerodrome that is just as it should be.

We taxi to the sheds and inspect their accommodation. There are many large hangars on this aerodrome. We do not need anything like all of them, so that we can spread ourselves comfortably.

The village also makes a good impression; all its houses are intact. The war has left no signs of its ravages here. Large farms occupy the outskirts; they have been turned into a milk depot. There are many cows in the stalls; landsturm men are milking them and making butter and cheese. This is a pleasant state of affairs, and one that promises all sorts of good things for the future.

There are good billets for our men. Large rooms are available for our depot and workshops; they have already been used for similar purposes. We only need to carry on the work that the former occupants have left off.

Our mess is a small villa near the aerodrome. Everything in perfect condition, with a large diningroom, readingroom and veranda. On the first floor I have my own quarters, a sittingroom and bedroom. Wart comes up to me, wagging his tail; he has already found a corner for his own particular resting place. My things have been put out on the writing-table, my trunks are unpacked and my uniforms hang in the wardrobe.

It is just like entering one's old rooms after returning from a journey. Where the Staffel goes, there my home will be.

We are free till the afternoon. For the next couple of hours it is impossible to find any pilot; they are all arranging their rooms and making themselves comfortable. Then, one after the other, they gravitate towards the mess with beaming faces. I have to inspect all their quarters, and am glad to see that they are all in luck's way.

Our cook brings in the soup; the first meal steams on the table. Over our coffee we hang the maps on the wall, mark in the aerodrome and draw the lines that represent the front and the boundaries of the sector.

The cables are laid and the telephone installed. Now we are in touch with the world again, and our life runs in its old course.

29.8.18. The weather has deteriorated. Many clouds hang in the sky, forming thick blankets over wide stretches of it. Flying activities are therefore somewhat curtailed. The centre of the battle has shifted southward; the official communiqué reports heavy fighting at Nêsle and Noyon.

31.8.18. The weather is very bad now. Yesterday we only got occasional glimpses of the sky through gaps in the clouds. Heavy mist and fog hindered visibility. Today there is a cloud ceiling at one thousand five hundred metres. No aircraft activity reported.

I go up alone to survey the situation. It would be pure waste to let the Staffel take off.

It is not pleasant flying under a cloud ceiling. One imagines oneself in a room and fears to knock the machine against something.

I climb up into the clouds with the intention of coming out on top of them. Dark-grey wet swathes of mist whirl by me. The air is as damp and oppressive as in a vault.

It grows lighter. I soar aloft; the ceiling lies below me and my wheels appear to be rolling on the clouds as on a field. But even up here the view is not clear. A second ceiling hangs high above me, while balls of cloud sail through the space between. Not a sign of the sun anywhere.

No machine about up here. I must be just about over the front, and so throttle my engine to glide down again. Perhaps I may find some English balloons up; they would be easy to attack to-day.

The air grows grey around me once more, and then I see the dark mass of the land looming up. The wooded patches near Remy are directly under me, and out to the left of them runs the great highroad. Here too there are no machines about, but over in the south-west—I can scarcely trust my eyes—there is a captive balloon! It hovers there, only a few hundred metres below the clouds.

I may succeed in surprising it.

I climb up into the clouds again and steer a course towards it. I can throttle down my engine, as I do not need to gain further height. This makes my flight easier, and the cloud ceiling sucks up all the sounds. They will hardly hear me, and they cannot see me because I am flying in the clouds and see the ground only as a blurred mass.

There is a light south-westerly breeze. I must therefore approach the balloon from north-east, so that it remains in my sights for the longest possible time if it is hauled down.

I fly in a westerly direction, following the road, and turn south-west when over Guemappe. Many villages pass by below me. I climb up into the clouds again, for in those villages there are many human beings, many watchful eyes that I do not wish to see me. I fly for a while by my compass; then I glide down slowly out of the clouds.

A village looms out of the grey. That will be Boiry; behind it runs the highroad from Amiens to Bapaume. The next village beyond is Boyelles, and there—huge, wet and yellow—stands the captive balloon.

Open up the engine and at it!

A swift glance round the sky; no protecting machine to be seen. Then my nose goes down towards the balloon and my machine guns hammer away.

I cannot see the balloon's car anymore, but two dots detach themselves from the monster and plunge into the depths.

Two huge white points suddenly appear in the air,—like shell-bursts. They are the parachutes that have opened to bear the balloon's observers safely to earth.

The dive sets my machines guns firing at lightning speed. The target is immense; not one bullet can miss it. I see them hit the balloon's taut envelope, like hail-stones pattering against a sail. When I am just over the balloon, I pull my machine up.

The balloon refuses to catch fire. I go into a turn and attack it again. The same negative result.

The balloon has been hauled down somewhat, and now I catch sight of its guards on the ground. A couple of shots cut through my wings, and I make an effort to gain the shelter of the clouds again. My way up has been lengthened somewhat, and the Archies treat me to a liberal helping of shells.

At last I am back in the protecting grey. I go into another wide turn and peer out below me.

The balloon is not on fire; it has been hauled down and is now quite close to the ground. I have no idea why it would not blaze up. I fired off about four hundred shots. Perhaps there were too few incendiary bullets among them.

Nothing more doing. I start off home, flying cautiously along the edges of the clouds, and it is not long before I am over the lines again. The clouds are hanging still deeper now, and several of them are discharging rain-showers. I fly round these wet walls and soon land on our aerodrome.

1.9.18. We are to have more new machines. Everyone is pleased, especially the pilots who have not yet got their Fokkers. But their joy is soon damped down, for the machines allotted to them are not Fokkers, but Pfalz D.12s.

What is a Pfalz D.12? No one has ever heard of such a machine, no one knows anything about it.

We decline to take these machines. The result is a series of long telephone conversations; we are told that they are very good, better than Fokkers in some respects (eyewash!), and we must take them. There are no more Fokkers to be had, and in any case these new Pfalzs are better than the old Albatroses, and when new Fokkers come along, we can take them in exchange.

All right; then we'll have the Pfalzs.

We go along to the park and take over the machines. The sight of them does not inspire much confidence; the fuselage and controls are the usual kinds, the wings are somewhat compacter, with a multitude of bracing wires. The whole contrivance looks just like a harp. We are spoilt for such machines, because we are too much accustomed to the unbraced Fokker wings.

Each of us climbed into the new machines with a prejudice against them and immediately tried to find as many faults as possible. The Staffel's opinion was the same as ours. The works sergeant grumbled because of the trouble the bracing was going to make for him while the mechanics cursed because of the extra work to assemble and dismantle them and declared them awkward to handle. No one wanted to fly those Pfalzs except under compulsion, and those who had to made as much fuss as they could about practising on them.

Later their pilots got on very well with them. They flew quite decently and could always keep pace with the Fokkers; in fact they dived even faster. But they were heavy for turns and fighting purposes, in which respect they were not to be compared with the Fokkers. The Fokker was a bloodstock animal that answered to the slightest movement of the hand and could almost guess the rider's will in advance. The Pfalz was a clumsy cart-horse that went heavy in the reins and obeyed nothing but the most brutal force.

Those who flew the Pfalzs did so because there were no other machines for them. But they always gazed enviously at the Fokkers and prayed for the quick chance of an exchange.

5.9.18. A cloudless summer day. We are in the air from dawn till dusk. The enemy is attacking all along the line and puts up strong aerial forces. We fight with scouts and double-seaters and attack the bombing squadrons making for our hinterland. We can dare more now, even though we are outnumbered, because we have good machines.

At night we sink down on our beds, dead tired.

On September 7th our retreat to the Siegfried Line is to begin. All the ground we won in the spring must be given up again. Will this retirement help us like the other one did? Will the enemy launch his attack against empty air and waste months bringing up reinforcements and making preparations for a fresh offensive? Shall we be able to strengthen our front in the meanwhile?

A dangerous storm is brewing in the west. Clouds, bearers of evil, are rolling together.

8.9.18. Rain is pouring down. Shreds of clouds scud by so low that they touch the trees and houses. A cold wind sweeps across the land. The battle is stifled in the ensuing morass. All flying washed out.

10.9.18. Once more we have to surrender lorries for troop transports. The weather is terrible. I ride up to the lines to discuss various matters with the formations in front of me.

Cambrai has been evacuated.

At Iwuy we meet the first fugitives. A long, black column of civilians. Their vehicles are two-wheeled carts, packed high with all sorts of household goods. Then there are small carts drawn by men and dogs, old people hobbling along on sticks, children with solemn eyes and weeping women—a long, black column. The inhabitants of the villages through which it passes stare at the fugitives, to whom they offer help and refreshments.

Cambrai has become a battle area. Perhaps the inhabitants of our village will soon be forced to leave their homes and farms and seek help afar from strangers. The nearer we approach to the town, the thicker the crowd becomes. In the suburbs of Cambrai the masses are blocked, like a flood by a dam, and the streets are choked up.

We have to go forward, and yet cannot use brute force. An old man pushes a crippled wife along in a hand-car. Sick people hobble on sticks along the rough cobblestones. At a crossroads a car lies in a ditch, with a broken wheel; all its contents are strewn in the mud. Two weeping women stand by it; a man stares helplessly at his household goods and then glowers at us with rage and hatred in his eyes.

What misery and distress are to be seen on these roads!

But sheer necessity compels us to evacuate the inhabitants. Cambrai has become a battle area, and already the English shells are hammering at the houses of the suburbs.

The town itself is now empty. The only beings we see are stray soldiers who are assisting the work of evacuation. Men are carrying huge bundles of documents from the town-commander's headquarters and loading them up on to lorries. Such a mass of papers has accumulated, and now it must all be taken back somewhere. I fear a lot of the stuff will have to be left lying there.

The streets of the western suburb are dead. Not a single soul is left to tread them.

The air is cleft by something that gives a mighty gurgle, and then a shell hurtles into a house with a huge roar. We hear a sound of crashing and bursting; tiles rattle down from the roof, a couple of beams come tumbling into the street. A swarm of startled pigeons circles round in the air and comes down again behind the gables with flapping wings.

Then all is quiet once more.

A curtain flutters out through a window, like a flag signalling the garrison's surrender. The walls of the houses throw our footsteps back with an eerie echo.

It reminds me of the days at the beginning of the war when patrols rode into a village. The same uncanny silence, the same waiting for something to happen.

A cat runs across the street and tries to gain admission by a closed door. She miaows for a while and then disappears down a cellar opening.

Another heavy shell hurtles along and falls somewhere among

the houses. The shells now fall at definite intervals—the minute hand of the war-clock times them.

The minute hand of the Cambrai town clock moves slowly towards twelve. Then the clock stops.

We overtake the refugees on our way back. Many carts have stuck or are being unloaded. The sides of the roads are strewn with household goods. They are worthless articles, mainly old junk, but for a time their owners dragged them along. Here lies a pile of books, there an old family portrait, and over yonder a gilded bridal wreath. Trifles, and yet to each of them is linked a heart, a memory, a slice of life.

The last refugees are the oldest and poorest. They have packed only a few oddments on their aged shoulders, and hobble on their way with tired feet. There is no life in their gait; they just shuffle through the mud along the road.

We have packed our lorry with as many as it can take. We have driven much misery on its way. Next to me sits an old woman, huddled timidly in her corner. She shivers as she wraps her old wool shawl about her lean body. In her hand she clutches a picture, the only thing she could rescue, the only thing that represents the sum of her many years. It is a photograph; a young man in French uniform.

Underneath it a quavering cross has been drawn in ink, with a date and the single word: Verdun!

We carry the refugees a long way past our village; then we have to turn back. An old man comes up to me. He speaks no word, he only stretches out his hand to me—a withered bony hand that gives hardly any pressure when it rests in mine. Two tears roll down on to his beard. Then he stands with his kindred by the roadside.

12.9.18. The front line runs through Arleux, Sauchy-Cauchy, Marquion, Moeuvres and Havrincourt. We have gained a brief respite by the retreat, but the enemy is pressing hard at our heels.

There are very few machines in the air. Only a few English two-seaters, that grope forward cautiously, endeavouring to reconnoitre our front line.

The sky is full of thunderstorms; there are clouds at all heights. Visibility is bad; a clammy veil lies over the ground.

We cross the front at Palluel and try to take the reconnaisance machines in the rear, so as to cut off their retreat. The enemy Archies are very effective to-day, but then we are flying very low, at about two thousand metres, which makes it all the easier for the gunners to find the range. Haze and clouds, however, afford us continual shelter and mask us from their view.

We overhaul an R.E.8 over Cagnicourt. Schmidt, who is nearest, attacks him. The Englishman makes off with all the speed he can muster, but Schmidt hangs on doggedly and refuses to let him out of his sights. The Englishman goes into a series of zigzags and then down in steep spirals. He bashes his machine into the ground somewhere between Riencourt and Quéant; what a pity he is on his own side of the lines!

Further southward we pick up two contact patrol fliers at a low height. They have not noticed our approach, even though it is embellished by a very long tail of Archie's shell-bursts. At last one of them sees us and clears off, but I catch the other over Havrincourt. He goes into a steep right hand turn, hoping to gain a passage to the west. But it is too late; we are too close on to him. He comes nicely into my sights; I have plenty of time to judge the distance. My guns begin to shoot—a series—then another—my tracer bullets give me the direct line to the pilot's seat.

The English machine heels over suddenly and goes into a spin; the pilot cannot catch it again, and so it crashes on the railway line near Hermies.

And doesn't this make the Archies wild! Machine guns on the ground also rattle away at us. Naturally we have to show some appreciation of their attentions; the air is clear, and as we have dropped pretty low in any case, there is no reason why we should not drop right down and pick out a few ground targets.

A large patrol has taken refuge in a hollow near Pronville, while round about Buissy there is a line of sharpshooters right across our course; a battery is firing from Brioche Ferme. Our rays of fire strike out in all directions, causing widespread destruction. Not a man of those snipers remains visible; all of them who can still run have taken refuge behind the walls.

We fly back at a low height above the highroad, jumping over houses and avenues of trees. The Archies have ceased fire; they cannot touch us when we are so low down. The machine guns on the ground have likewise stopped because we are out of their range.

13.9.18. The same picture as yesterday. Only a very few English contact patrols flying at the front.

This time we surprise a D.H.4 over Recourt. The fight is a short one; we emerge suddenly from a cloud, and behold, his cockades are quite close to me. The observer has hardly time to turn his guns on to me before his machine goes down in a spin and crashes. A few seconds later its wreckage lies on the ground.

We pay another little visit to Brioche Ferme. The guns are not close to the houses today, but on the brink of a ditch a little distance away. We have only time to fire a few bullets into the shellhole in which the khaki uniforms crouch; then we pass on.

Close to the first houses of Villers-les-Cagnicourt stands an armoured car belonging to a mobile anti-air-craft battery. It is a particular pleasure to put a few shots into it. You'll get your revenge another time, Mr Archie, when you'll be able to plaster the sky with shell-bursts without having to fear any retaliation from us.

Jagdstaffel 23 comes to meet us, and we join forces to hunt a contact patrol flier, who clears off in a hurry. Then the haze swallows the last remnants of visibility and the clouds melt into rain. Our work is finished for the day.

14.9.18. We are not to fly to-day,—not even in our periods for free hunting. The order has gone forth that His Excellency General von Bruck will inspect Scout Group 8. The Staffels are to hold themselves in readiness. Further orders will come in due course.

We pull all our machines out of the hangars and range them up on the aerodrome in one long, straight line. There is much difference of opinion about the correct attitude for the propellers. Some of us want to see the blades in a vertical position, which would give the most orderly appearance, but others prefer to have them placed horizontally to the ground that this attitude is more suitable for a long line and does not break the view. There appear to be no regulations dealing with the point.

I ordain that the propellers shall be placed diagonally so as not to side with either party. Diagonally, from left to right downwards; this presents the smartest appearance. Like a cap at a rakish angle over one ear or a flower in the buttonhole. The others see the point and agree with my view. Yes, yes, we have our little worries.

It was not quite so simple to get all the propellers fixed at the right angle. The compression had a word or two to say about the business and generally put up an obstinate resistance at the last centimetre or pushed the blades too far over. But at last we got them all in the desired position and felt inordinately proud of the good work.

A day of feverish activity for the Staffel. Everyone was polishing or scrubbing or whacking something. Almost like the day before a peace inspection.

The sergeant-major has two deep furrows between his eyes and plays at being in a bad temper. The N.C.O.s, who are otherwise always on the friendliest terms with their men, are continually cursing and raising objections to something or other. Mindful of my own days in the cadet school, I also play the martinet.

The men are lined up in two ranks in front of the machines. Before them stand the N.C.O.s, and in front of these the pilots. I parade up and down the lines, uttering platitudes about the correct positions for caps and sword-belts. I curse loudly at slovenly neck attire and fingers that do not touch the trouser seams as they should. In short I rage around like a war-god.

The men are delighted because they realise that my bark is worse than my bite. They know their Staffel-leader too well.

Everyone has done his best to show the Staffel off in a good light. One of the N.C.O.s is even wearing a pair of gloves—white kid gloves, with three black stripes down the middle fingers. Lord alone knows, where he got them. He is particularly proud of his smart appearance and most injured when I tell him to take them off. After all, we do not need to look too pretty.

At last a group of officers approaches the village. I cannot put spurs to my horse and gallop up to them, for the simple reason that I have no horse. I therefore walk towards these gentlemen.

I salute and report; we shake hands. Then His Excellency passes along the ranks with me. I introduce my pilots and explain the types of their machines.

There is no need to be afraid of this inspection, because the general is not an angry martinet but quite a paternal old gentleman. He shakes hands with one and chats with another; he knows that they are all doing their best. He has not come to find fault, but only to have a look at us—like a father visiting his children. We all feel that and welcome him warmheartedly.

What is the good of insolence from above, any way? It cannot impress us; we only laugh at it and think our own thoughts.

What is the good of inspections? Anyone can put a top polish on accoutrements that are so rotten inwardly that they positively stink. What is the use of finding fault with things that cannot be changed one jot?

Just hot air!

It is far better for a superior officer to treat us in paternal fashion, knowing that his subordinates are his children.

The Staffel is dismissed. We remain on the aerodrome with the general, chatting about various little matters. Suddenly a telephone message for an escort comes through. Staffel 32 is on duty and takes off.

The machines muster over the aerodrome and fly towards the front. The general waves to them, and then stands gazing after them.

For a long while he remains with eyes turned westward, although the last machines have vanished in the evening sky some time ago. He does not say anything to us about flight formations or battle duties, but merely breathes the wish: "I hope they'll all come back safely!"

15.9.18. To-day our forces are counterattacking along the Arras-Cambrai road. Time and scope of the attack have been communicated to us, together with a sketch of the enemy's positions. Our job is to keep the air free so that our ground fighting Staffels can do their work without interference.

The morning begins with a drizzle. It is not the right sort of weather for a battle. But gradually the clouds rise and it grows lighter.

We take off at 10.45 a.m. The rain has stopped, except for a few local showers. The clouds have coalesced into a closed ceiling at about one thousand metres up.

We soon reach the front. A German fighting squadron flies over the lines, but there are no English machines visible anywhere.

I hang about for a while and then fly across the boundaries of the sector, but it looks as if the English do not mean to show themselves to-day. The Archies are in for a fine time because we are flying so low, and blaze away for all they are worth. The air is free; we can join in the battle down below. As the fighting Staffel is flying south of the road, we will look for promising ground targets on the north side. I notice that most of the shells are bursting in the meadows along the Agache valley; that is where the lines will be.

We are now quite low down and can distinguish the German and English steel helmets plainly.

English infantry stream out from Rumaucourt and try to advance. We turn our fire on them and drive them back under cover of the houses. Away to west, behind Saudemont, we then sight a huge infantry column on the march. A big, attractive target. They hardly have a chance to see us; they are completely taken by surprise when we float up over the housetops and pepper their ranks. They break up in frantic confusion, and make a forward rush for the shelter of the houses.

Three times, four times we attack this target; then we pull our machines up again and fly on. A wide turn takes us back to the lines. Everywhere we see khaki troops—everywhere good targets. At Buissy we turn our guns on to some thick masses of reserves.

Now we are over the main fighting zone again. The force of the bursting shells sets our machines swaying and dancing.

We find a battery firing from the western edge of Baralle. We surprise its gunners; they have no time to take cover. They just sink down behind their guns. Behind some gardens horses are waiting to pull the guns away. Glancing eastward I see the helmets of field-grey troops at no great distance. If we can stop the limbers reaching the guns, our infantry will capture the battery.

Just a fraction of a second to consider the situation—then I put my machine into a turn and fly towards the first team. The gun-carriage and its six horses loom up and grow in size with eerie swiftness. I bend over my sights. Two, four, six horses, brown shining coats, intermingled with a couple of khaki figures, small, bent figures—their drivers.

Two, four, six heads, tossing up and down—quite big heads now. But when I am a couple of metres above them I whirl away and zoom up in a turn. My finger did not press the trigger-button; I could not bring myself to fire at those horses.

A thousand thoughts flash through my brain.

It is so easy to kill a man. He is armed with the same weapons as I am, he knows what he is doing, and he has the same chances as I have. We have to kill men in war. War may be mad and wrong, but it is war. There is some purpose behinde very war, even if it does not emerge clearly enough to be understood by everyone.

But what does an animal know of mankind's wars?

What do horses know of the battle?

They are only victims to be slaughtered in the interests of mankind. Their deaths are unjust.

Once before I killed a horse. My own.

He was wounded when I was out on a patrol in Russia. He carried me out of range and then collapsed.

The wound was a bad one. It had torn the animal's body up, and there was no chance of saving him. He lay on the ground quite quietly; I knelt beside him, drew his head to me and stroked him. His eyes gazed at me, with huge pupils that conveyed a look of such inexpressible sadness. A faint rattle escaped the body that quivered in pain.

Only a rider knows what a faithful friend his horse can be to him. Only the man who has ridden to a war knows what it means to lose this friend. I stroked his skin and gazed into the great eyes— indifferent to anything that might be happening around me. If Cossacks had come along to capture me, they could have shot at me to their hearts' content; I should not have noticed them. The world around me was non-existent. The death-rattle grew louder, and the convulsions that racked the body ever more painful.

Then I drew my pistol from the holster. The cold metal was icy to my hand!

One shot! The life faded out from the great eyes. My own eyes stared into emptiness.

And so a thousand thoughts flash through my brain while the

battle rages beneath me and my machine is tossed hither and thither by the eddies.

If the battery gets away, its guns can fire on our soldiers again—can wound and kill them. It lies in my hand to prevent this. I must prevent it; I am under orders to prevent it. I am a soldier and must obey.

I see that the first gun carriage has already reached the guns. It has turned about, and the men are dragging a gun up to it. I put my machine into a steep turn and fly towards the group. The team comes into my sights—two, four, six horses, with the short bluff noses of the Norman breed, noses that sniff the air—my finger falls from the trigger-button and my machine whirls onward.—over their heads

Great horse eyes stare up at me. My brain is bursting with the thoughts in it. What is the matter with me? Will not those guns have to stay there in any case? No, they will get them away.

It must be done.

Another turn—another approach. My machine guns rattle away this time. My glasses cloud over, so that I have only a blurred view of a mass of kicking hoofs and rearing bodies.

Then all is over, and my machine tears off westward. My guns are firing away, but my thoughts are not on their targets.

On our homeward way we pass over the position of that battery again. I see the abandoned guns, and beside them lies a limber with six dead horses, a little further away another and by the side of the road yet a third. With each limber there is a great brown mass—six dead horses.

Grey, steel-helmeted figures loom up by the guns. A wave of snipers goes forward to occupy the shell-holes and ditches that face the enemy. Our infantry has captured the battery position. As we whirl over it, the men wave up to us; joyful faces shout greetings.

The counter-attack has been successful, and we have contributed our share towards the victory. We practically captured an

English battery. It is a wonderful victory—fine enough to be mentioned in the official communiqué.

But I have no joy in it. I can still see two great eyes—twelve great eyes. I have committed murder.

The weather has cleared up suddenly. A fresh east breeze has chased the clouds away, and it was not long before all that remained of them were a few little balls on the horizon. A clear, pure sky smiles down on us.

That caused flying activities to develop to their full extent. The front reports the presence of strong English squadrons. The Staffel is ordered up at 5 p.m., and we fly to the lines with nine machines. On our way we see an English squadron of many machines making for our hinterland, but we cannot get at them as they are flying far too high.

Wings gleam out all over the front. Just as we are flying over Baralle again I see a scout squadron of seventeen machines directed towards our lines—Sopwith Dolphins, S.E.5s and Sopwith Camels. They are about two hundred metres below our height; we go into a turn that will bring us out with the sun at our backs. The air above us is clear; this time we are the highest machines.

We approach the Englishmen. They fly on a straight course, having apparently failed to notice us as yet. I give the signal to attack; our noses dip, and down we go in a steep dive. Schmidt on my left seems to be in a particular hurry to-day; he is flying at almost the same height as my machine.

A Dolphin comes into my sights. He does not notice my approach, as he flies straight on, unconcerned. One hundred metres—eighty metres—fifty metres, now my guns begin to shoot—thirty metres, the Englishman sideslips and then goes down by the nose. His wings flutter and break away. He disappears into the depths below me, and suddenly I find myself in the midst of his companions.

The dogfight begins. Schmidt is sitting on a Sopwith, while Stoer and an S.E. go into turns. The others are engaged in a tail-chasing bout with the rest of the English. A Sopwith in front of me tries to dodge my guns by a turn; I hustle him away from his formation and begin to shoot. Turn—a series—turn—another series. I cannot get him while he is in his turns, but my bullets rattle round his ears when he flies straight for a few moments in an effort to rejoin his crowd. At last he has enough and goes down in a spin. I cannot follow him down because the fight absorbs my entire attention. I have to rescue Marx, who is hemmed in by three Englishmen and hardly able to defend himself.

The fight brings us considerably deeper; we attacked at four thousand seven hundred metres and now we are down to two thousand. Gradually the mêlée breaks up; the English fly off westwards, and we rally over the lines.

All the nine of us are there, but four Englishmen lie down below. The fragments of my first victim, the Dolphin, are scattered over a wide stretch of ground.

The English working machines have made off at the same time as their scouting squadron, and now the front is free. We fly up and down the sector for a while and watch our own machines spotting for artillery. Then we turn home again. There is no sign of the bombing squadron, but away to southward a veil of Archie's shell-bursts hangs in the sky. Probably the bombers have taken a different way home in order to avoid us.

We land; the news of our four victories spreads quickly. All our men have beaming faces and perform their wonted tasks joyfully. The mechanics inspect the machines and fill them up with petrol, the armoury sergeant and his assistants supply the machine guns with fresh belts, while the shop sergeant ascertains the damages and gets them repaired.

Little Meyer comes running up, out of breath. We always

allow him to write our combat reports, and he has to keep a book about the condition of the machines, with a tally of all losses or additions. He runs so hard that his cap flies off; he does not stop to pick it up, but just runs on. He has heard of our success, and is beaming all over.

"All right, Meyer, write it down!" I dictate the report: starting time, landing time, weather, visibility, highest altitude reached, etc., etc., the fight with the English scouts. Special remarks: 7.5 p.m. one Sopwith Dolphin shot down by Lt. Stark in territory west of Bar-alle, 7.10 p.m. one Sopwith Camel shot down by Lt. Stark, 7.8 p.m. one S.E.5 shot down by Lt. Stoer, 7.6 p.m. one Sopwith Camel shot down by Sergeant Schmidt. Detailed report follows.

"That's all."

"Oh, lovely!" slips out of Meyer's mouth. A most unmilitary expression! A criticism on his superior officer which must not be allowed to pass, even if kindly meant. But it is a long time since we regarded ourselves as soldiers here; we are just one large family, and what harm is done when the youngest of us gives vent to his delight?

I pat Meyer's rosy cheeks, give a tug at the hairs of his blonde head and dismiss him. He does a sturdy right about turn, follows it up by a jump into the air like a young foal, and away dashes the blonde little bullet.

The boy can run. He has a good time with us. He is a mere child, but he joined up voluntarily. As he is interested in technical subjects, they sent him to the sappers first, but he was not strong enough for the strenuous work there, and so he came along to the Air Service.

One fine day he turned up at our place, delighted to be out at the front at last. He has an easy job here; he just has to lend a hand where needed, and manages to make himself useful. He is our re-port-clerk and telephonist; in his spare time he sits at the telescope and searches the sky for enemy aircraft. He is in luck's way, for he is in the war and yet far from the firing line. He is a piece of youth that will not be sacrificed.

How many of his age sit in the trenches? How many of them lie under the soil? Youth—lads of seventeen—our sunny youth!

But what are we? Only a few years older. When the war began we were only seventeen, but we fought. We marched, rode, fought and bled.

We are not much further on in years now. But we are so old. We no longer belong to the younger generation. We are old and young together. Our faces are still smooth, but one has wrinkles round the eyes, another a sad drawn expression about the mouth and a third deep furrows on the forehead. Not all—many still remain unmarked. But one thing we all have in common, one thing that we shall never lose—the serious look about the eyes.

The eyes have seen too much suffering. This suffering has passed into the soul and cannot be rooted out. In the eyes it takes the semblance of an invisible veil.

16.9.18. To-day I sit sadly in my room, staring out at the evening sky. My left leg reposes on a chair; our ambulance N.C.O. is putting a thick bandage on it. I got a scratch on my last flight; nothing serious, just a graze on the shin. I need not go to hospital; I can stay with the Staffel.

We took off at noon; once again we shot up trenches and battery positions. Then we did our second patrol in the late afternoon; there was much flying activity, and we had several fights. We could only send up five machines because the others had sustained slight damage and had to be made serviceable again.

We met an English crowd over the lines. They were numerous and aggressive; we had hard work to wriggle our way through them. Three were sitting on my back, while two others potted at me from the sides. A couple of bullets splintered something in my cockpit;

then I suddenly got a frightful bang on my left leg. The force of it sent the stick over to the left; my machine went into a sideslip, and so I came clear of further bursts.

I went into a turn and gradually wormed my way out of the scrap. I felt a severe burning pain in my leg, although I was able to move the muscles. I decided that it could not be anything serious!

But the pain increased and prevented me from using my rudder. I saw I was not much use at the front and flew home. Meanwhile the others had found their way to me and formed up in their regular order.

I first thought of firing off a red light to signify that I was going to drop out and let someone else take the lead. But I turned it down because I realised that four machines were too weak a force, and in any case petrol was running short, so that we were bound to go home soon.

The result is that I am sitting here, contemplating the damage. The wound has stopped bleeding and does not hurt so much now. The only risk is that inflammation may set up.

I have got away with it pretty well. Wart is with me, sniffing at the bandage from a respectful distance. He turns up his nose sharply when he smells the iodine and sneezes a couple of times. Then he looks at me reproachfully, as if to enquire what are these malodorous things which master has wrapped round himself to-day.

Yes, yes, my dear dog, you don't always smell of roses.

To-day I have plenty of time to polish off all the office work. My office-sergeant is delighted because I have to sit still for once in a way and listen to all he says. Every cloud has a silver lining.

Chapter *IX*
IDLE DAYS IN THE VOSGES

17.9.18. All sorts of things are afoot. Our people are continually standing about in little groups to talk and guess. We are going to make another move. Orders have come to pack up everything and dismantle all the machines, including the Fokkers.

What are they going to do with us? So far our sector has been the busiest part of the front. We are needed here. The enemy's numerical superiority is large enough as it is; how can they possibly send three Staffels away? Where are we going to? Nowhere in this neighbourhood, for then we could have flown to the new aerodrome. It is very perplexing.

I hobble about with a stick and superintend the work. I do not notice my wound much now. On the one hand I am rather glad that the move is curtailing our flying activities because it is better for me to rest my leg, but on the other I cannot quite get the idea of it into my head properly.

In what theatres of war could we be needed? Somewhere where we have to go by train—not Russia or the Balkans. Italy? Perhaps!

We talk and speculate and find no enlightenment. Italy? The idea is taken up at once; naturally, it can only be Italy. We get hold of maps of that part of the world and talk it over and paint rosy pictures. It is autumn up here; a trip to the sunny south would be just the right thing for us.

A SUCCESSFUL SURPRISE ATTACK FROM
THE CLOUDS ON A BRITISH RE 8.

By evening we have got most of our packing done, so we indulge in beautiful visions of our future until the small hours.

18.9.18. All our machines have been dismantled, including the Fokkers. The fuselages stand in the sheds, with their wings leaning up against them; they look very fat and sleepy. They are like chrysalises hanging in some sheltered spot to await the time of their reawakening.

As we have no machines to fly, all our martial activities are suspended. All at once we have become gentlemen at large.

We have packed all our baggage, and that finishes our work. What are we to do with ourselves? The only thing we can do is to drill the men; this would bore us considerably and them still more. There would be no sense in it. At present we hardly notice that we have time hanging idle on our hands because we are sufficiently occupied in speculating about our move and trying to guess its riddles.

24.9.18. It is almost incredible. We have been kicking up our heels beside our dismantled machines for a whole week, looking on idly while fierce battles are raging at the front and our people are short of machines. We must sit still and watch the English bombing squadrons come across daily and drop their eggs in our vicinity. What is the matter? Have the authorities forgotten us?

We are none the wiser, even if we ring up a hundred times a day. We merely receive the answer that our order to entrain may come any moment.

This waiting is terrible.

We make trips in the immediate neighbourhood, but there is not much to see. The district is more or less bare, and the villages all look alike. But even if they had been beautiful they would not have pleased us because we are so bad tempered that nothing can be right for us. We have had a lot to swear about in these last few days.

The town of Denain affords us some sort of diversion, as a German theatrical company is playing there every evening. Good plays, well acted, and a very pretty theatre. But after the performances we hardly allow ourselves time to drink a glass of beer in some hotel. We hurry home as fast as we can in the hope that our marching orders may have arrived. But we get no further than hoping.

We really do not know what to think. Have the military authorities so many aeroplanes at their disposal that they can afford to dispense with a whole scout group?

25.9.18. I was playing with the idea of taking the responsibility of having a couple of Fokkers re-assembled, but to-day our orders came at last.

Our train stands ready for us at a siding in Bouchain station. As it is not a long way from our place, we made quick work of the loading up. Our machines are already on their trucks—two to a truck. With their bare struts pointing upward and outward, they look like antediluvian monsters. The train gives a jerk and moves on a few metres so that fresh trucks can reach the siding. Our lorries roll on to the train and are made fast; finally the passenger accommodation comes along.

It is a long train. We do not need all the coaches and wanted to have the superfluous ones taken off. But it cannot be done; so and so many coaches were ordered, and so and so many must travel with us. Well, all right!

We found we could spread ouselves to our hearts' delight. As we had plenty of time, we turned our conveyances into a 'train de luxe.' The truck with our cars on it is coupled next to our living coach, so that we can use it as an observation carriage. Beyond this are the kitchen and canteen coaches.

Our paymaster has turned an ordinary cattle-truck into a nice private apartment for himself. His bed stands in one corner, with clean sheets and luxurious skin rugs; his writing table is on board, with all its accessories, as well as an armchair and a table, on which are vases containing fresh flowers. The walls are hung with rugs and decorated with a number of pictures. He has even fixed up a small stove. This room aroused universal envy; we considered it fabulously luxurious—good enough for the boudoir of some wealthy beauty.

Then came our electric light machine—that is the greatest joy of all. Every coach is connected up with the electric current and provided with bulbs, so that they will all shine in radiant splendour. The long cables that stretch the length of the train arouse the displeasure of the station officials, but that does not worry us. The main thing is that we are supplied with excellent light. We proudly spurn the proffered tallow dips which make feeble efforts to shed a dubious light on the interiors of the ordinary transport train.

At 6 p.m. we are ready to depart. Lieu St. Amand looks down on us from the hill on which it stands. Our sheds are empty, and once again all stability is removed from our lives. Already we can hardly realise that we lived up there for a brief space of time.

At 6.15 we hear the signal to depart. At the very last moment my dog jumps out of the train and tries to make for his old quarters. For some reason or other he has not forgotten them as quickly as we have. The reason soon becomes manifest. In the field near the siding stands a little spaniel bitch, wagging her tail. She is Aimée who lives in a house next to our mess, and Wart is very much in love with her.

With a bark of delight Wart bounds up to his lady-friend. They begin a series of joyous games, frisking up and down in the field as if there is no such thing in the world as a train that wants to start off. Whistling and calling has no effect, and it is not so easy to catch the animal. But at last we get him into the compartment and tie him up to a leg of the seat to make sure that he does not escape again.

Aimée stands on the platforms and gazes up sorrowfully at our window. Then she draws breath; when she sniffs the smoke of the engine, she turns away slowly and trots home.

The train is moving. Whither? Whither? Great is our suspense this time.

It is still fairly light when we start. At present we are making for Valenciennes. An English bombing squadron is flying high above us. Not a rosy outlook for us, because these raiders often make railway lines their targets, and unfortunately we are sitting in a train instead of our machines. It would be extremely unpleasant if they dropped anything on our roofs. But the English-men disappear into the distance and our train rolls on its way, bearing us to more peaceful country.

From Valenciennes we bear eastward in the direction of Mons. This tallies with our speculations. Night falls, and as we know that we cannot change our course for the time being, we settle down to sleep. The coming day will give us further particulars.

26.9.18. The morning shows us a large town with walls and fortifications, with towers and stately houses—it is Namur.

Where lies the way to Italy? Southward! Correct! The train bears off to southward.

It wanders through the beautiful Meuse valley towards Dinant. We bask in the glorious sunshine in our cars and enjoy the view. Rochefort. Libramont. Arel. Luxemburg. Diedenhofen.

The day wanes, and once again it is evening.

At last, on the evening of the 27th we reached Metz. Before we got there we stopped at a provisioning station—at Woippy. They call it Wappingen now, but they are a bit late with the germanisation of such names in Alsace-Lorraine. They had forty years to do it; now, I fear, it is too late.

Just as we rolled into Metz station the warning for enemy aircraft was sounded. In the twinkling of an eye all the waiting rooms were emptied, and their inmates made a bolt for the cellars. We and

THE LAST LIGHT OF THE SETTING SUN CASTS
ITS RAYS ON THE END OF A FIGHT.

our train were left abandoned and deserted in the wide, wide world, but the enemy was kind and refrained from unloading his bombs on to us. But the shell-bursts of the Archies made a great row in our vicinity.

We grew bored in time because we could do nothing but wait. So our orchestra struck up a tune. The sweet melodies soon enticed various people out of their cellars, and when someone broached a cask of beer in our canteen-coach, things began to get lively in our part of the world. Quite a number of people collected round the train, but it was not long before a station-master came along and cursed us for disturbing the traffic. He was very peeved at our gay life.

We stayed so long in Metz that we began to get afraid that they would detrain us there, but at last we carried on. Meanwhile we manage to collect some news about our destination. We are not going to Italy—unfortunately. We are near our journey's end, because we are going to settle down somewhere in these parts.

What on earth is happening here? We are not particularly pleased with the prospect, and there is much cursing from those of us who were dreaming too intensely of flights in Italy's blue skies. Well, tomorrow we shall know definitely.

28.9.18. The train stops often and for suspiciously long periods. We are somewhere near Saarburg. At last we draw up at a siding. The adjutant of our group welcomes us with the news that we are to detrain here.

We have no notion what we are going to do in this part of the world. Neither side has started an offensive here; it is the quietest part of the whole western front. But orders are orders, and so we begin to unload.

First I get a car taken down and drive off in it to glean some definite information. In Saarburg I meet the commander of our group, who gives me the necessary details. We have been sent here to lie in wait for the big bombing squadrons that fly in to Germany almost every day. Our aerodrome is to be the parade ground at Bühl. No billets have been fixed up as yet, but we can make arrangements for ouselves at Bühl, Schneckenbusch, Mückenhof and Neuhof. We shall have very cramped quarters because the villages are small and unpretentious. None of them contain any big buildings. We search the map in vain for a chateau.

I obtain the southern portion of the aerodrome for my Staffel and Schneckenbusch for our billets. Schneckenbusch* and Mückenhof—the names do not inspire much confidence, but we must see the place before we start cursing.

I drive back to the station and send off an advance fatigue party. Then we set off for the new aerodrome.

It is a huge place. One cannot see across it. At one end there are a large number of wooden sheds. It is impossible to count them, but there are enough to house twenty Jagdstaffels.

The northern edge is occupied by a Bavarian Staffel that has been here for some time. We greet old friends and gather some news about the district. What we hear does not sound very promising; there appears to be practically no enemy aircraft activity in this part of the world. The only machines that come along are the bombing squadrons that visit Germany, and they fly at an enormous height. The aerodrome is quite a good one, but it often gets bombed. Which is not unnatural, we all think, because everything can be seen quite plainly, and all those many sheds simply ask for bombs. When we move on, we discover quite a number of bombholes, and, judging by the size of them, we decide that they give us quite a pedigree sort of prize bomb here.

Schneckenbusch is an insignificant village, with dirty houses, but it lies in quite pretty surroundings close to the Rhine-Marne Canal. We start off with a row with the inhabitants. They are an

Literal translation: Snail-bush and Fly-farm.

OPPONENT UNDER FIRE FROM THE PALE
THREADS OF TRACER BULLETS.

impudent set of fellows who do not want to give us a single room; then keep on protesting that they are German subjects, and yet they speak practically nothing but French. We soon settle them, however, by annexing all the very best rooms in the place, and they can complain away until they are blue.

We have got to look after our men first and foremost. So far we always managed to get on all right with the people in France and Belgium on whom were we billeted, but we are not going to argue with this mob. So much the worse for them, of course, because they might have had all sorts of advantages if they had been nice to us.

29.9.18. So once again we are busy getting ourselves shipshape. It takes a lot of work, as we have a long way to carry everything. The mechanics are making the machines serviceable, and everyone else has something to do.

While this work goes on, I drive round the district with our group-commander to look for further possible aerodromes. The scenery is pretty enough, but there are not many spots for an aerodrome, because it is all hilly country, even mountainous in places, with lots of woods and watercourses. But our trips are glorious; it is autumn, and all the woods are decked out in the appropriate colours. The architecture of the houses often reminds me of our own villages, and as quite a number of the inhabitants speak German, it is just like being on a holiday excursion at home.

1.10.18. We make our first trial flights and take a look round the district.

The Rhine-Marne Canal runs direct from east to west. Half way to the front we pass the big fish-ponds at Godrexange; then come a lot of woods. The front lines are close to Parroy, whence they turn south east towards Blamont.

Nothing to be seen in the air—not a single machine or balloon. A sad sort of place for us; we are most depressed and curse all day. We talk things over with Captain von Schleich and tell him that there is no use for a Jagdstaffel here. He agrees with us and admits that he did not want to have us. But then he smiles mysteriously and hints that things may be different soon; we must just wait and trust him. If Schleich says that, it must be all right. We venture to hope again.

3.10.18. We got the big surprise to-day.

Orders from G.H.Q. arrived to the effect that a Bavarian Jagd-geschwader No. 4 was to be formed of Staffels 23, 32 and 35, with 34 as the fourth Staffel. The Squadron-leader is to be Captain von Schleich, and we must reckon with another transfer within the next few days.

Great was our joy when this good news came through.

We fly to the front. When we get to the fish-ponds we test our guns. There is a little island in one of the ponds—or rather, a patch of reeds. This serves as a target, and we can see the effect of a burst very well in the surrounding water. A lot of ducks flapped off when we came along.

Nothing doing at the front. Not a single machine anywhere. The huge forests completely mask the life on the ground below us; here and there an occasional trench peeps out to betray the fact that there is a front line. We were not, however, particularly interested in discovering the lie of the front because we are going to be trans-ferred again soon and so do not need to get used to things here.

Many of Archies cloudlets are bursting around us. The French gunners have one thing in common with their English brethren; they love to plaster a whole sky with shell-bursts.

Lunéville lies below us—old memories of 1914! There is Vit-rimont Wood where we lay while they pounded us with heavy ar-tillery; there is the road to Einville along which we rode and Raville sur Sanon where we had our billets.

A delicate breath of autumn lies over the land.

We fly home again. It is idiotic to waste petrol here.

The canal snakes along below us like a broad, shining ribbon.

I drop right down and skim the waterway as I fly eastwards. La Garde lies before me. Here the Bavarian Uhlan Brigade rode to the attack on August 11th, 1914. Here is the wide field that slopes down to the canal, with its yellow soil that rang to many thousands of hoofs, there is the corner of the wood where my own regiment captured the guns—the first guns captured by Bavarian troops during the war. I fly over the bridge that saw so much bloodshed and over the houses of La Garde where the charge was checked. In those days we were boiled in the summer heat; the light flickered on the hilltops and the wide cornfields were a golden-yellow waving mass, ripe for the sickle. But now the breath of autumn hangs over the land, and all Nature lies in deep peace.

I circle over the field. I drop right down. Under the trees I see a monument that was not there before. It is wrought of huge boulders, and on it is a tablet. "Here sleep seven Bavarian cavalry officers."

Chapter X

FIGHTING ON A WAVERING FRONT

4.10.18. The enemy has started his great offensive along the whole front. There is fighting everywhere between the sea and the Meuse, but Cambrai still remains the principal battle area. This has hastened G.H.Q.'s decision to send us up there again.

Our marching orders came this evening. We began to dismantle the machines at once; our men were working feverishly all through the night.

5.10.18. The leaders of the various Staffels were summoned to meet the squadron-leader. "How do you think it would be if we flew to our new sector to-day?" he asked. "It will be quicker than going by train, and we can look around for aerodromes until the Staffels arrive, which will save much waste of time."

An excellent idea! Flying is far more comfortable than rumbling along the rails. And if we are lucky, we may catch a bombing squadron on the way.

We agreed upon the hour to start. Schleich, his adjutant and the leaders of the other Staffels came along to me about noon, and we took off for the north at 1.15 p.m.

It was a wonderful flight. We did not fly high, only at about one thousand metres so that we could get a good view of all that was taking place on the ground. It was a pure joy to see our five machines glittering in the air under the rays of the glorious sun. We flew in very close order and pointed out to each other the various beauty spots on the ground over which we passed.

We steered a northwesterly course. First came vast forests, with huge ponds and lakes. Then we passed Bensdorf junction, after which a mighty river gleamed on our left. It thrust itself ever nearer to our line of flight until a great town loomed out of the grey mass of haze—Metz.

Onward, north-westward! To west of us rises up a ridge of delicate colours, which keep us company for a long while—the Côtes Lorraines. Then another great river comes up to us—the Meuse. We follow its course and land at Mouzon. Here is the aircraft park belonging to an army corps, and we can fill up with petrol.

Then we carry on. The green woods of the Ardennes rise up ahead of us on our right; below us large towns are dotted along the Meuse valley like pearls on a string. Sedan, Charleville. The Meuse worms its way northward through the heights of the Ardennes in huge bends and vanishes from our view at Fumay.

There are still great forests to our right, but on our left there lies wide open country. Rocroi, Hirson, Avesnes.

Now a great highroad runs due north to Maubeuge. We have already reached a district that is familiar to us from former times. Bavai lies before us like a mighty star. Nine straight, wide roads meet here, making the place an unmistakable landmark.

We land on an aerodrome at Bavai and put our machines in the tents. The group there lend us a car, and we drive straight off to the army H.Q. at Quesnoy.

We learn there that the situation is not particularly hopeful. Our retreat still continues; strong enemy forces are at our heels. The firing line runs just in front of Cambrai and Douai; we must look out for aerodromes that are well in the rear, somewhere about on a line between Mons and Thuin.

It is too late to do anything to-day. We look around for quarters, but the place is crammed full. At last we get an attic, where I have to share a narrow bed with Seywald, the leader of 23. A most uncomfortable night; we have only one small blanket, and it is decidedly cold. We gradually warm up again in the morning with the help of hot coffee.

6.10.18. Eight hours continuous run in a car. We try all over the district, but it is not so easy to find aerodromes here. The country is thickly populated, and there are practically no big fields. Everywhere we go, we run up against huge farms with fences and ditches and gardens which would delight the heart of any peasant but only depress us.

A brief rest in Mons. Here we can still get all sorts of things to eat, and we do ourselves well. Then we resume our hunting, but cannot find anything suitable.

Back again to Quesnoy, where we creep into our cold beds.

7.10.18. We were luckier to-day. We have found aerodromes. They are certainly small, and will need a lot of things doing to them, but at least we have reached our goal. We cannot accommodate all four Staffels at the same place; the 23rd and 32nd must go to Harmignies, while the 34th and 35th are berthed at Givry. All arrangements have been made, and the billets are practically given out. We can do nothing more at present except await the arrival of our Staffels. We drive to Mons and stay there because we can get decent rooms and need not freeze any more.

8.10.18. The group that is looking after our machines has been moved back, so that we must take them elsewhere. We fly them to Maubeuge, where we hand them over to another group, and then decide to stop there ourselves. An uncomfortable state of affairs; we do not quite know where we belong, and we begin to miss our luggage because we have only the barest necessities with us.

The weather has turned bad; it is foggy and a light rain is falling. I only brought a mackintosh with me, and have caught a bad cold during the trips in the draughty car. I have a sore throat, and my temperature is up. But I cannot be ill now, and so I drag myself about until I can stick it no longer.

10.10.18. I am lying in bed in Sous les Bois, a suburb of Maubeuge, where I am billeted on a French family. I feel terribly lonely. If only the Staffel would turn up soon!

I am so weak that I can hardly lift my arms, and yet I am possessed of an unrest that seeks to drive me onward.

Day and night I hear the tramp of marching columns; they are all going back. With them are long trains of wagons and crowds of refugees who have been evacuated from the front and are drifting eastwards. The further we are forced to retreat, the larger these masses of fugitives will grow.

My fever conjures up all sorts of visions. I imagine myself left alone here, to be found by the enemy.

I have nothing to complain of here, however. The French family nurse me with a care that is really most touching. They bring me all sorts of things that do me good or give me pleasure—wine, fruit juices and books, but refuse to take any payment.

The old man often comes to sit by me and tells me many tales. It is only natural for us to discuss the war; the Germans are retreating; any child can see that, and it is no use trying to conceal the fact. Every day the refugees bring fresh tales of disaster; the French are said to have broken through at Le Cateau, and English cavalry have reached Lille. The old fellow is delighted at his countrymen's successes, but does not let me see his joy. He only talks of war in general as a great calamity; moreover he is afraid the fighting may spread to here. He is deeply attached to the home he has built up out of his savings with such great labour, and his eyes gaze sadly on the various objects in my room.

The future is so full of uncertainty. War is a great misfortune.

12.10.18. If only the Staffel would come! This waiting is intolerable.

In my room there is a map of France and Belgium, on which my landlord has drawn the front lines. It looks just like our own maps, but naturally he looks at things from the opposite point of view. He draws thick lines in ink—always more and more lines to eastward, and each of them is marked with a date.

On the 10th he drew a ring round Cambrai. The town fell that day. Yesterday he marked off a big stretch of territory on the southern part of the Front—the French were in the Chemin des Dames sector. To-day he has drawn a line eastward of Laon. How does the old man get such accurate news? His lines are always correct. They leer at me from the wall, writhing their way into my brain like black serpents.

This evening I had a visit from Seywald, who told me that the Staffels will arrive to-morrow. He will send my car for me when they come. At last! I am so happy that I have only got to stick it another night.

13.10.18. I am waiting in my room, all ready and dressed. My temperature is normal again, but I feel very weak, and my legs shake when I try to walk.

Suddenly the door is pushed open forcibly; Wart rushes in and nearly tears me to pieces with joy. Then Weber, the driver, comes for me and takes me down carefully to the car. He has brought my fur overcoat and a lot of rugs, which he wraps lovingly round me. Stoer and Ach have also come along; they give me the news of our Staffel. But nothing special happened; the journey went off without a hitch.

14.10.18. We are billeted in Givry. It is raining, and a cold wind sweeps down on us from the north, pushing grey clouds over the land and pounding the fog into thick masses. Deep furrows of mud have formed on the roads, and when we cross the meadow that constitutes our aerodrome, water squeezes and oozes up so that every footstep leaves a miniature lake behind it. But it is just the right sort of weather, because it gives us comfortable time to assemble the machines.

Close to the aerodrome, from which it is only separated by the road, there is a large, spacious villa, surrounded by a pretty garden. One might almost call it a chateau. This is our mess, and here we all have our living quarters as well.

Jagdstaffel 34 has arrived and found quarters not far from our own. I had a joyous meeting with some old comrades, but many were missing from whom I parted so lightheartedly in Foucaucourt. I also saw many new faces—the faces of men I did not know; they are the replacements for my old friends. There are many strangers in 34—too many for me.

Püt and Kithil are still with my old Staffel. I had a long talk with them, for we had much to tell one another. Almost every sentence began with: "Do you remember—" and then we nodded our heads and said: "Yes, those were great times."

Meyer, who was always so lucky, has been shot down in flames. Lieut. Bauernfeind was reported missing one day, and nobody heard anything more about him. Dieterle was wounded, and is home on leave. Schmidt had a lot of victories and is now leading a Staffel somewhere in the Champagne. And so it goes on.

All their lives are different, and yet alike in the main outlines. Flying—always flying and shooting down opponents—sometimes many victories and great successes—and then the story ends with a last flight, a fatal battle and a crash.

That is the way we all end; that is our common lot. One is given a long lease of life, another finds his end almost at the beginning. But one and all finish up the same way.

16.10.18. I received information from the flying school that my old observer is there, waiting to be seconded. Dear old Helmo—so he has managed to get to the school, after all, and now he is through and wants to join my Staffel. I am delighted at the idea of seeing him again; I have not heard anything of him for a long time.

The flying school has also been moved a long way back, and is now located at Nivelles. But it is not so far from here, and so I fly off to pay Helmo a visit.

I find the usual activities going on in Nivelles. There are many machines standing about on the aerodrome; they are continually taking off and landing. A swathed figure emerges from one of them, a long fellow who is much too long for the small single-seater. A never-ending leg comes out, followed by another, and I simply cannot understand how their owner found room to stow them away.

Then the figure comes up to me, pulls the leather helmet away from its face, and there is Helmo grinning jovially at me. We wrung our hands in a long fervent grip.

Then I went straight off to the office and put in my application. All the formalities are through, and Helmo can join us in a couple of days. We'll have a lovely time then.

17.10.18. The little town of Binche is not far from our aerodrome; it lies about ten kilometres due east. My squadron was quartered there in the winter of 1914. We spent Christmas there—a jolly time on which I like to look back. I decide to have another look at the place.

Nothing has changed; I remember every house. The only difference is that it looks more lively; various columns that are quartered here fill the streets with their activities. In the old days it was a quiet, dreamy place, still just a bit startled by the beginning of the war.

I pull up before Monsieur Junot's house. We used to buy our wine from him in those days; he often came to a meal in the mess and entertained us in his house. We got on splendidly with him.

"Hallo, bon jour, monsieur, how are you?"

"Bon jour, monsieur, what can I do for you?"

"Don't you remember me?"

"No, monsieur."

"Well, just have a look at my uniform—green trousers with the broad red stripes—Christmas 1914."

"Oh, mon Dieu! Oui, les uhlans bavarois! Le monsieur Stark! Oh—quelle joie!"

He calls out to Madame. She prepares a meal and fetches the best bottle from the cellar; then we start to talk. M. Junot remembers everything that happened in those days; he recalls all our names and asks after their owners. He knows that my old captain is dead—he heard it by chance and assures me that the whole of Binche was sad when the news came through. All the inhabitants have such pleasant memories of those days; when we left a Prussian Landwehr company came in our place, and they did not get on so well with them.

Junot made me go along with him to visit quite a number of people, all of whom greeted me cordially. We also looked in at the pub where we drank many an evening glass; we had our tree there on Christmas day. The landlady has grown somewhat stouter; her eldest daughter has married and lives in Brussels, but otherwise there is no change.

"Where is Jeanne?"

Jeanne was a dainty, blonde lass. She was just the right sort of innkeeper's daughter, and consequently the recipient of much poetic devotion from us. I was head over heels in love with her—from a distance, of course. I was so happy when I got a chance to talk to her and in the seventh heaven when she shook hands with me at parting. At night her vision was often in my dreams, and those dreams were frequently daring and unrestful. But that is what happens when one is only just seventeen, when the heart is opened like a flower and thoughts buzz about in it like the bees in springtime.

Jeanne came in and—nearly threw herself at my neck. She remembered only just in time that there were other people present.

We talked over old times until the lateness of the hour compelled me to go home again. I had to shake many hands, and many good wishes and much advice went with me. I was told to be careful with my flying and keep myself safe. "And come and see us again when the war is over."

Yes, when the war is over . . . what will things be like then?!

Goodbye, all you dear people!

For a long time Jeanne stood waving to me with the handkerchief, on which she had dried a couple of tears. For a long time I saw that handkerchief as a white point in the grey evening.

20.10.18. Various pilots have joined the Staffel, and gradually we have crept up to our official strength. Helmo Ludovici is there; he is to fly a Pfalz D.12. The rudder-bar had to be pushed forward to accommodate his long legs. I am jolly glad to have Helmo in the Staffel.

Lieutenant Hess came the day before him, bringing with him a cheery optimism and a thirst for mighty deeds. He wanted to fly off and shoot down a victim at once, but it was not quite so simple a business as that because Hess is a raw novice, with no experience of the front. I had to break him in to his job gradually.

When he realised that it was not quite so easy to shoot down an opponent, he wanted to have a go at a balloon. But I could not let him do it straight off, because an attack on balloons must depend on various circumstances. I dared not allow him to go blindly at one of them; it would have meant his certain death.

Hess did not understand that. He cursed a lot, and was really wild with me. That is the spirit I like to see in young pilots; I would rather have them too headstrong than too tame. We can make something of Hess.

The additions to the Staffel made us a very large table in the mess. We found ourselves short of plates and dishes, so we all subscribed a few marks apiece and decided to get a new set.

We went off to Mons one day when all flying was washed out. We soon found a suitable shop, the owner of which was delighted at the chance of selling us something. He has got the wind up about the enemy's shells and fancies they will smash all his goods to smithereens. He is looking for trouble rather too soon, but his idea is right, for shells and chinaware do not get on well together. We got a lovely dinner service out of him very cheaply and carried it triumphantly—though carefully and slowly—home.

Our table was set for a banquet that night. The new china positively shone; our mess orderly gave himself extra pains to polish it all up and even went so far as to embellish the table with flowers and greenery. The illumination was supplied by candles in a heavy silver candelabra. The only things lacking were dress clothes and ladies.

We could almost forget there was a war on that evening. A couple of beech logs burnt in the open fireplace, and the flickering, crackling fire gave the room a warm, cosy atmosphere. We lounged in soft armchairs and behaved as if the world was at peace.

We heard sounds of laughing and singing from the kitchen. Our batmen feel very comfortable here; they were not long in making friends with the servants in the house and even got a couple of them to help. One man chops up wood for them, while another cleans the boots; in return they give these Belgians cigarettes and other luxuries and spin them yarns startling enough to make the joists of the house curl up. Although the two parties do not speak one another's respective languages they have established an excellent understanding.

Ah, there is nothing like a cosy evening round a fire!

Crash! Bang! A fearful din startled us from our comfortable ease. Outside a woman's voice screamed loud—then there was silence. I rang the bell to enquire what was the trouble and then, with a foreboding of some dreadful tragedy, I got up and went out.

A buxom peasant girl whirled past me and shot out through the kitchen door into the open air. Then I saw that the kitchen floor was strewn with fragments of crockery. Our new dinner service was completely wrecked.

Schlüssler, the mess orderly, stood over the ruins like a weeping willow, gazing sorrowfully at the mess with half a tureen in his hand.

"Well, what sort of a pigsty do you call this? What's happened?"

"Beg your pardon, sir, but we'd just washed up and put everything on the tray. The girl from next door gave us a hand, and then she seemed to step on something that wasn't there, and down went the tray."

"Indeed. I should have thought you'd have been the person to step on something that wasn't there—not the girl. Anyhow, for the future you can do your work without extra help; I won't have any more civilians in the house. And certainly not any girls."

And so one buys some nice things, only to have them smashed at one fell swoop by an ass like that. Our lovely new service has gone to the devil. Cursing won't help; it won't mend it again.

A soldier should never give his heart to toys. From tomorrow onwards we shall eat our meals off the field-kitchen's tin plates.

21.10.18. The weather has not changed much. Whenever we flew to the front in the intervals between the rain, there was not much to be seen. The whole sky was covered with a thick mist.

Our sector is much the same as the old one, except that it has been pushed a bit further eastward. Bavai is our landmark, as there is a straight road thence to Givry, and another just as straight that leads to Le Cateau. This latter highway simply can't be missed because it skirts the edge of a huge forest. This is more or less the southern boundary of the sector; northward our territory extends as far as Valenciennes.

We often met English machines and had a few fights with

them, but generally we were alone in the air and could hardly find our way about. The country seems to have grown much wider, and it gives us a feeling of desolation.

The front line runs along St. Amand, Denain, Solesmes and Le Cateau, but you can hardly call this a front. Rearguard actions are continually taking place in open country, and the enemy wins a victory every day. We lost Ostende on the 19th, and on the 20th we gave up all the coast line.

G.H.Q. wants to make a new front and mass troops behind it. The line they suggest runs from Ecloo to Deinze, Tournai and Valenciennes; they talk of it as the Hermann Line and hope to hold up the enemy's advance there.

We flew about in the bad weather, but did not feel happy. We never knew exactly where our own troops were, but noticed the fact at once when we crossed the enemy's lines, because we always came under a very hot fire. The homeward flight was often difficult; the clouds hung right down to the ground, so that one could hardly find one's way about. We were always glad when we reached Bavai and could grope our way home along the road.

22.10.18. Rain. Having orders to protect a reconnaissance machine, we fly round the Valenciennes district with it. The ground below us has become one big lake, as it is flooded far and wide. Dirty, grey masses of water that reflect only dismal clouds, lie leaden and inert beneath us. Our job was soon over; we ascertained the presence of numerous reserves on the enemy's side. Very few enemy aircraft about. On our way home we shot up the outskirts of Solesmes, where we found strong enemy forces.

23.10.18. Our front has wakened up to a big battle again. Valenciennes is the centre of heavy fighting.

We took off three times, and found quite a number of aircraft swimming in the misty air over the battlefield. We had a good many scraps with enemy scouts, which could not prevent us from chasing several of their two-seaters away.

One Englishman was forced down. He hovered over a flooded meadow for a long time; then he put his machine down on the water like a duck, and it turned over. It must be most uncomfortable to drop down into cold water now, but, after all, flying is not exactly comfortable work at present.

The sun seems to have disappeared for good. The wet wind makes me shiver, and the cold eats into one's very bones. No light falls on us from above; below us there is only a dead, grey land.

Below us the retreat is going on.

We are no longer in touch with our own troops; the only communications that reach us are brief orders. We feel ourselves deserted, and it grows lonelier around us every day.

We no longer believe in victory, but we are still hopeful. We are still deep in the enemy's land, and a retreat is not the worst that could happen. We may be able to make a stand somewhere and build up a new front line.

We have not lost the war yet. We hear of mutinies in the French army; we hear of peace offers and peace aspirations.

But we also get news that our own troops are nearly finished. Letters from Germany tell of mutinies and plans for revolution. We know nothing definite about these and do not want to believe in them. We just carry on with our flying and fighting.

We are alone in a world that we do not understand—a world that is changing around us. We no longer believe in victory, but we still cherish hopes.

The sun has set in grey mists.

Chapter XI

IS IT THE END?

2 4.10.18. Columns march into Givry. Tired, worn-out horses trot along in front of the wagons and stagger when they come to a halt. The drivers grumble when they unharness them and go to look for accommodation in barns and stalls.

The front continues to move eastward, the retreat is going on. The first of its outlying spurs have reached us.

More columns loom up in the mist and roll by us, away into uncertain distances. The mud in the streets smothers all sounds; we can bear neither the creaking of the wheels nor the beat of the horse-hoofs. The mist spews up colourless forms and then swallows them again. They pass by us like a army of ghosts and disappear into the grey. The retreat still continues.

We also have received our orders to retreat. Once again we must look for an aerodrome. It is more and more difficult to find one, because we are moving back into a huge industrial area. The country here seems to be one large town.

After a long hunt I find my Staffel a decent aerodrome at Gosselies. But even here we have a lot of preliminary work to do. Our advance fatigue party goes off, and the removal follows its usual course.

We meet the base once more at Gosselies and promptly have

173

a row with them. Close to the aerodrome there is a small chateau, which I marked down as quarters for the Staffel. It possesses the great advantage that we can house all the pilots under one roof, so that it is easy to get in touch with them for emergencies.

Of course there happened to be a number of big base officers living in the place. There were a number of billets in the town that were just as nice, but the base-wallahs refused to change over; they were deaf alike to polite requests and urgent demands. One can only wonder at the thickness of their skulls; they seem to think the sole purpose of the war is to give them the chance of being kind to their stomachs in luxurious quarters.

Thank heavens, I only needed a single conversation over the telephone with G.H.Q. to put the matter right. Then an order came along that the base-wallahs were to clear out of any billets we needed. They were simply blue with rage when they pushed off.

We don't care. We have no pleasure in such triumphs, which are trivial matters for us. We have no more time for that sort of thing.

26.10.18. At last the weather has cleared up. The sun shines in the heavens, and there are only a few clouds to cast their shadows on the ground.

But all of a sudden it is autumn. The air is different; it contains the cutting cold of winter. Visibility is misty; the haze, however, is not the summer's dust but the coalescence of strips of fog. Not long ago the woods were full of greenery, but now they lie all red and yellow beneath us. The big forest near Bavai lies on the ground like a vast sheet of copper; at its edges where a couple of water-courses still keep the meadows green I seem to see great patches of verdigris. The autumn landscape below me is either brown or dull yellow.

The battle round Valenciennes is still raging. We find enemy aircraft at all heights there. Strong squadrons fly across into our hinterland; there are many airfights. The enemy's numbers are increasing every day.

EASILY VISIBLE SPOTTER BALLOONS MAKE FOR A
VERY TEMPTING TARGET IN THE CLEAR AIR.

THE VIEW FROM "THE DRIVER'S SEAT." THE ENEMY IN THE
SIGHTS SEEKS TO SAVE HIMSELF BY BANKING STEEPLY.

28.10.18. Our move is finished. It was more difficult this time, because it gave us a lot more work to dismantle and reassemble the tents. Many of our lorries have broken down with the continual strain imposed on them and are at the park for repairs. We have very little transport at our disposal.

But at last we have got this move over and fixed every thing up at the new aerodrome. We have struck lucky with our billets. The house is a clean but unpretentious building, with two huge side-wings that give us a lot of space. We have refrained from oc-cupying the principal rooms of the castle; it would have been a pity to do any damage to those gorgeous apartments with their smooth, polished floors and valuable furniture. There is a lot of rare china about them, and many precious pieces of bric-à-brac on the walls. We have therefore installed our mess in the coachmen's quarters, where everything will be more practical and comfortable for us.

The chateau is surrounded by a park that contains a lot of old trees. Some of them are already quite bare. Two great beeches hang over a pond, trailing their branches in the still water. Their foliage that drapes the ground is blood-red.

The reports we receive from the front are always scantier and vaguer, but we know that all our front-line from the North Sea to Verdun is giving way. We are fighting rearguard actions everywhere. G.H.Q. has devised a new line on which we are to make a stand; it will be along the Meuse, or perhaps even further eastward. We still get the official communiqué in the evening; every evening we learn that more ground has been lost. Then we draw new lines on our map and mark the date.

When we take off in the morning and fly over the ground where the front lines ought to be, according to our map, we see English troops below us and know that our men have been forced to give up yet another piece of ground.

We have grown very lonely; in fact we feel that we are super-fluous. The group does not even call on us for escort duty now;

the reconnaissance machines seldom take off because there is nothing for them to do. There is nothing more to reconnoitre and no spotting to do for the artillery. Likewise we are unable to help our infantry because we never know their positions. We feel that the end is near, but we dare not speak of it.

30.10.18. Splendid weather. The mists are gone; even the smoke from the Charleroi chimneys has dwindled to thin wisps. From early morning onwards the air resounds with the whirring of propellers. Mighty squadrons pass over into our hinterland and plaster the whole district with their bombs.

We were lucky enough to catch one of these squadrons over Mons. It consisted of two flights of seven and ten machines, with an escort of fourteen scouts flying above them. There were seven of us, and we soon found ourselves mixed up in a furious dogfight with the English. Their scouts stayed up above instead of coming down to help the two-seaters; why, we could not imagine. We managed to force one flight to turn back, but the other tried to push past us towards Mons. However we caught them too, and they retreated when we sent one of them down in a spin, with smoke pouring from him. In fact the English showed little of the fighting spirit to-day that we are accustomed to expect from them.

The field-post brought us a huge consignment of letters and newspapers in the evening. Formerly the army postal arrangements worked without a hitch, but now it seems to have become very irregular.

In my budget there was a letter written on dainty paper. For a long time I held it poised in my hand. When I opened the envelope, faded petals fell out—dried asters.

It is autumn, and somewhere at home a beautiful woman has plucked her asters. But there was also a linden bud between the sheets, and the written lines bore a message of hope and yearning for the spring.

A hope of the coming spring—born in autumn. One day the

OBERLEUTNANT VON GREIM, OF JASTA 34 WAS THE FIRST
TO SUCCESSFULLY SHOOT A TANK FROM THE AIR.

gloom must pass, and a new age will be born—an age that is as
golden and smiling as the spring.

But autumn is around us. Only autumn. This will be our last
autumn; then comes a winter which will be our end and our grave.

My fingers stroke the faded blossoms. The petals break off
and sink to the ground with a sigh.

Everything has its end. For us there will not be another spring.

1.11.18. A cloudless sky and a clear view. Lively flying activities
at the front and numerous enemy squadrons coming over. The artillery fire round Valenciennes has stopped, but there is a huge con-
flagration to be seen there, and black clouds of smoke ascend to

heaven. It seems to be a munition dump that we have destroyed or the enemy has set on fire.

The columns of smoke form huge craters in the air. I can see them over Valenciennes, Le Quesnoy and Avesnes, but the largest of all comes up from Maubeuge. The smoke rises straight up in thick pillars to about one thousand metres, where it continues with a slight westerly slant to fifteen hundred. Its further progress up to three thousand metres is subject to a sharp push to northwards; then it spreads out in all directions to form a huge flat ceiling. A mighty phenomenon that holds its place in the sky for a long time. Towards evening the fires increase; red flaming points glow up everywhere.

At night we receive news that Valenciennes has fallen. All over the place our people are destroying munition dumps so as to prevent the enemy from turning our own guns on us.

4.11.18. No communiqués came through to-day. We have no idea what is happening at the front.

From the air we saw all the roads crowded with columns of men marching back. Then came an area where everything seemed to be quiet, and beyond it we saw other columns, strong and numerous columns.

The war seems to have stopped. It is quite a rarity to see the cloud of smoke from a shell-burst.

Plenty to do in the air, but not so many bombers coming over. We have a number of fights with enemy scouts and two-seaters, but score no successes.

When we come down, we find columns marching past our aerodrome again, and infantry detachments have been quartered in our neighbourhood. A Prussian flying group is sharing our aerodrome and has put up its hangars close to the road.

We have received orders to stand by for another move back. We are ready for it, because we unpacked only the barest essentials. All the same we shall hardly be able to manage it this time, as practically all our lorries are out of action. The new aerodrome is to be at La Bruyère, about twelve kilometres north of Namur. We send off an advance party of N.C.O.s and men as usual.

6.11.18. The enemy has bombed heavily all the roads along which our men are retreating. He also bombed our aerodrome, but did not do any damage, except to a lorry of ours that happened to be on the way from Charleroi to Gosselies. It was touched by a couple of splinters, which inflicted slight wounds on the two drivers.

9.11.18. Another large slice of territory has been lost. Ghent, Audenarde, Tournai and Condé have been given up; the enemy has also occupied Bavai, and the front line now runs through Avesnes to Marle. The news from the southern parts of the front is likewise unfavourable. The enemy is in Rethel, and Stenay has fallen. But we have no time to worry about such matters; we just carry on with our flying and fighting.

So the enemy has taken Bavai already! I see the town and its many roads lying beneath us like a spider in his web. It always seemed such a peaceful place but now it stares up at us with an aloof, hostile air.

We have a number of fights to-day, mainly with scouts. All types of aircraft are represented at the front—Sopwith Camels and Dolphins, S.E.5s and various two-seaters. We have leisure to observe them all. The S.E.5s are beautiful machines, but the Camels look very ordinary; there is nothing particular about them.

The Dolphins are really ugly; they are too big and lopsided. You could imagine that someone gave them a smack on the upper wings and bashed them in. But the S.E.5s look like birds of prey. When you see them circling round one another with their V-shaped wings, you could think they were real birds. Their slender noses give the appearance of birds heads thrust forward to peer into the distance. I always enjoy watching an S.E.5 in flight.

When about to turn homeward, I sight seven English scouts

over Bavai Wood, flying lower than us and in a southwesterly direction. They are S.E.5s; as they are directly over the dark wood, their ochre wings stand out in sharp contrast from the ground below. Their cockades shine like gaudy butterflies above the dark-brown background of dead foliage.

We dive straight down on to these English machines. They are flying straight home, having apparently failed to notice us. I get the hindermost of them into my sights and fire several series. At last it heels over and goes down in a spin, falling into the wood, where it is caught by the mass of branches.

Now the Archies assail us furiously and we make a bolt for it, as we are a long way in Tommy Atkins' territory. The twilight is also falling slowly.

Only 3.30 p.m. when we land, but quite dark. The wall of smoke from Charleroi hangs over the aerodrome and shuts out the last rays of daylight.

That was our last patrol.

10.11.18. A grey day dawns on us. The light cannot get through properly; thick blankets of fog and mist cover the sky.

Infantry and artillery columns are marching along all roads. They tell us that the retreat is still going on and that the English are not far behind . . . all vague rumours and chatter, mingled with insults and jeers, with curses and bitter scorn.

Our aerodrome is as quiet as ever; all our staff are carrying on with their usual work. This calm is most uncanny. We feel quite lonely and deserted; we know that we shall have to look after ourselves soon.

The telephone is not working. No news reaches us—no orders—nothing. I send an officer along to the squadron-leader with a request for instruction and accurate information. We await his return feverishly.

I tell the Staffel to stand by and give orders for our move to

BEFORE OUR LAST START—THE WAR IS OVER!

take place tomorrow. If we receive no instructions, we must act on our own initiative. We cannot stop here—no, not another day. We need clear roads for our transport, but the day after tomorrow they will be choked full of troops. We have no notion how we are going to get everything moved. We have only two serviceable lorries; we are been asking for spare parts for the others for ever so long, but no one sends us any.

We shall need a full week to get through the move with only

two lorries. But the enemy will be here long before the week is up. The position is hopeless.

Staffel 34 is quite close to us, just at the other end of the aerodrome. I go across and talk things over with Greim. But he knows no way out; Staffel 34 is also short of lorries, and short of petrol too. The lorry he sent to the park to get some returned empty. Thank heaven, I have a larger supply of petrol and can spare the other Staffel some of it.

No. 34 is also cut off from our commanding officer. Greim has sent an officer to squadron headquarters to get news. The worry of it all weighs down on us like a fog.

My adjutant arrives back about noon. The news he brings is horrible—it is the end.

Rumour and truth—complete break-down. Armistice, retreat to Germany. Mutiny at the base, the fleet under the red flag, soldiers' councils, revolution at home.

The Staffel receives orders to withdraw; we must at least try to save the machines. Perhaps we might manage to fly back to Bavaria and establish a frontier defence force there. We shall have to defend our frontiers against Italy; the Italians have crossed the Brenner Pass. We must start back as soon as possible.v

Chapter *XII*

THE END

I T IS the end! We are to return to Germany. The machines are serviceable, and we have enough petrol. So we can save our machines at least.

But the rest of our material? We have two lorries and two cars; that is all our transport. Hopeless to expect those spare parts now. What are we to load up? We can only take the bare minimum. What are we to leave behind then? Practically everything.

Our men are quiet. They carry on with their usual work; they do not want to know anything about mutinies or soldiers' councils. I have not many orders to give them, but each one does his job properly and willingly. The officers and men of my Staffel always got on well together; there is no reason for them to quarrel now.

We load up one lorry with the more important documents from the paymaster's office and mine, along with the officers' and men's baggage. The second lorry is reserved for valuable tools and instruments, some arms and reserve rations and petrol. The rest of its available space is to accommodate the men who are not fit to march. The cars can take hand luggage; Wart and my batman will also travel in one of them.

We can take nothing else; all the rest must be left behind. All the tents, most of the tools, the broken-down lorries, many arms—

the whole depot, in fact. We shall have to destroy the lot.

Our paymaster has a splendid idea; he wants to sell the stuff to the local inhabitants. Excellent; we shall at least get something of its value back.

So the paymaster instituted an auction sale, and there were really a few people who were stupid enough to pay good money for our things. If they had known the stuff will all be going begging tomorrow, they would certainly not have been so keen with their bids. The goods that fetched the best prices were a lorry-trailer and our copper telephone wire. But tools also sold well.

Tomorrow everything of value that remains over must be burnt. Then the machines will take off, after which the rest of the Staffel must start the homeward march.

The pilots have packed their things and seen to their machines. One after the other, they turn up in the mess and drop into their usual places. Our evening meal is served, but afterwards we remain seated round the long table and talk. It is the last evening we shall all be together; tomorrow is full of uncertainties.

The war is finished. That means the end of our flying. All of a sudden our strenuous activities are replaced by an empty nothing. Tomorrow there will no longer be a Jagdstaffel 35.

What will happen then?

We shall be scattered to the four winds.

"I shall go on studying and be an engineer," says Ludovici.

"Business for me. I shall go into my father's firm," says Stoer. "No fear. I could do that too, but I mean to stick to flying," declares Hess.

Naturally we all want to stick to flying. What else can we do? It is not everyone who can go back to college or enter a business which is waiting for him.

"Naturally we are all going to stick to flying," calls out Kranz, the little light cavalryman who joined us only a few days ago. He has only done a couple of patrols, so that the whole sky is still full of hope for him. Kranz talks away and tells us how nicely things are going to turn out for us. We listen and nod our heads assentingly and are glad to believe him.

"We shall all fly home and land at Schleissheim, where the Staffel will be reorganised. Then they'll send us somewhere on the Italian front. Or else there'll be peace, and we shall carry on with practice flights and squadron manoeuvres. The flights over the mountains will be the best of all. And then no more Archies, and the battles in the air will only be make-believe. We shall be quartered at Schleissheim; that's nice and near to Munich, so that we can often get there on leave. It will be a gorgeous life."

Our fairy tales are so beautiful that we almost forget the realities.

We stand round the map. We have actually had a report on the position of the front lines tonight. Whether it is true or not, we do not know, and as a matter of fact we do not care, but all the same I mark the line on the map.

Ghent, Audenarde—that is the old line. Then it bends away to eastward. Renaix, Leuze, St. Ghislain, Mons, Givry—our old aerodrome—Erquelinnes, Trelon, Liart, Mezières, Sedan, Mouzon, Stenay. And by the line I write the date: 10.11.18.

That was our last front line.

We stare at the map with vacant eyes. We cannot see the names and towns now—in their places the figures of the years rise up before our eyes—1914—1915—1916—1917—1918.

Five years! And every single day of those years filled up with names, figures and lines. And for every day of those years crosses rise up—many countless crosses!

That is how it was once upon a time—now it is all over. The lines are blurred, the figures reel and the names fade away. Only the crosses will remain.

Long, long they will remain.

But there will come a time when even the crosses will sink into oblivion. Everything has its end.

My fingers span the map and point our way to the east.

Tomorrow we must fly off. We have a long, long way to fly. Whither? We can remain just over a couple of hours in the air. How far can we get in that time? Where can we get fresh petrol? We have no idea where the aircraft parks will be, but they are certain to have moved from their old spots.

I consider it best for us to make an effort to reach Metz; the town is on the line of our homeward flight, and we are certain to get petrol there. Metz is somewhat near the front, of course, but it is a fortress and will surely hold the enemy up for a while. Also the neighbourhood of the front is not unpleasant to us, for the rumours from the base are not particularly alluring. It is not a long stretch from Metz to the Palatinate, and then we shall soon be in Bavaria.

We discuss all the possibilities for a long time. Let us hope there will be good weather tomorrow. Our gathering does not break up until the small hours, and then some of us still go on talking outside our bedroom doors. I let them go on talking—but things will not turn out as they think.

From outside the tramp of marching columns reaches my ears. A shuffle and a rolling—here and there shouts and abuse—and curses. Then the night swallows up the din, and the rolling mists bring fresh sounds to my ears.

Dead leaves, drenched with rain, flutter earthward to be trampled into the ground by many feet. The dead leaves never stop rustling down, and the tired feet never cease shuffling along the cobblestones. We are retreating! we are retreating!

The hours drip away and fade into eternity.

Autumn goes to her end—Nature is dying.

Winter is at hand—the grave.

There will never be another spring.

11.11.18. The last day dawns. My batman has called me early. It is is still night outside my windows, and thick swirls of fog steal by.

But already there is a bustle and stir everywhere. Points of light flit along the road and disappear among the houses. Then they reappear, linger a while and vanish again. I hear a murmur of voices and the sounds of trunks and packing cases being dragged along the floor.

The last of our baggage is going off.

We have breakfasted. Schlüssler packs the mess equipment.

The lorry stands waiting in the courtyard, and our batmen pile our baggage on to it. My big trunk finds a place there. In the course of time I have acquired a lot of property, and so my luggage has increased. I have a lot of valuable things in my trunk—all my many photos among them; their loss would be irreplaceable. And now all my effects are on the lorry.

Shall I ever see my things again? It is uncertain. Will the car stand the long journey? Will it be plundered on the way? It is all so uncertain.

The lorry is ready. Schlüssler puts the gramophone and its records on top of everything. He cannot bear to leave them behind. And they cannot do more than get themselves broken en route.

Now it is daylight. The fog has vanished, but the sky is still full of low-lying clouds.

The lorries rumble off to the mustering place on the aerodrome. Having nothing more to do here, we follow them. It is like a funeral procession.

On the aerodrome the mechanics are giving the engines their trial runs. I hear the brief hums and then the sudden whoops of the propellers—the old, accustomed, beloved sounds—to-day for the last time!

Our way takes us past the Prussian Staffel, and we greet their officers. I enquire when they propose to start their homeward flight. There is a look of sad despair in their eyes when they tell us that they cannot fly because their men have cut all the bracing wires and controls on their machines. It sounds so impossible and incredible to us, but it is the truth.

What has happened to our machines then?

They are all serviceable. Everything is in order. But our mechanics know all about those cut wires and controls. I ask why they did not serve our machines the same way.

That makes them really angry. How dare we think them capable of such a mean trick, they reply. Of course they are going to stick to us now, and if anyone comes across from the other formations and wants to destroy the machines, they are going to use their weapons on them.

We distribute all the uniforms and underclothing remaining in the stores among the men, and tell them to divide up the rest of the provisions and canteen stores.

The sergeant-major and his clerk bring along all the papers and documents that have to be destroyed. Soon a big bonfire flames up and reduces them all to ashes.

The Staffels form up. For the last time I pass along the ranks and gaze into the familiar faces. Suddenly my heart grows very heavy.

I speak a few words of farewell—not many, for the pain of it quivers about my lips and chokes my words. Then I shake every man's hand. Huge tears are running down little Meyer's chubby cheeks.

"Come on, keep your head up, my dear boy. You won't have any more reports to write for me now; you can go along home to your mother." Then I have to turn away; otherwise there will be tears running down my own cheeks.

The sergeant-major makes a speech and thanks me in the name of the Staffel. But I can hardly hear his words; only with difficulty can I control my emotions.

Then three cheers resound across the field.

I have given my last orders. Under the leadership of the adjutant and the sergeant-major the Staffel is to start the march home as soon as we have taken off. I have marked out their route; the rest must depend upon circumstances.

The kitchen car is attached to a lorry. It contains plenty of provisions, so that everyone's rations are assured for the march.

We don our flying kit and get ready to take off. Some of the pilots are hardly recognisable. They have all put as much as they can on their persons, so as to make sure of getting the garments home. Most of them are wearing two overcoats and possibly two jackets, as well as all the airman's usual extra clothing.

Their aeroplanes look more like beasts of burden than war machines. One has a trunk tied on to its under-carriage, another has a handbag buckled on to a strut. The cockpits are loaded up with all sorts of luggage.

Stoer is so small that you usually see very little of him when he is in the pilot's seat, but to-day he has grown a couple of heads taller, for he is sitting on three parachutes which he proposes to take with him. He has taken a great liking to these parachutes, because they are made of a very nice silk material; later he proposes to have them cut up and made into shirts. There's an epicure for you!

Gassl comes along to me with a complaint that his trunk is too heavy to go inside his machine.

"Well, why not dismantle your machine gun?" I suggest. "Or at least scrap your ammunition? Then you'll manage it more easily."

"But I am the pilot of a scout machine, sir. I cannot possibly take off without my gun and ammunition. No, the trunk will have to stay behind, then. It's quite likely we might meet some Englishmen."

We shall certainly not meet any Englishmen, and our arms are now quite useless. But I like to see my pilots show that spirit.

Schmidt, my faithful follower, is not with me this morning; he went off on leave a couple of days ago. Ludovici is to fly his machine, and Kranz will have Ludovici's. So now no pilot and no machine need be left behind.

The weather shows no signs of improvement. There is a thick cloud ceiling at five hundred metres. But we see Staffel 34 taking off from the other end of the aerodrome; there is no sense in waiting any longer. Everything is ready; I give the signal to start.

One machine after another taxies along the ground and rises into the air. Then a mechanic hurries up to me and reports that an engine is giving signs of trouble. So that machine must stop behind. Another goes over on to its nose when it tries to start, but the pilot is unhurt. Kranz is the last to start before me; I notice that his machine is rolling badly and beginning to stall; suddenly it goes into a sideslip and crashes. A complete write off. I climb out of my cockpit and sprint to the scene of the disaster, but just as I arrive Kranz crawls out of the wreckage and greets me with a friendly laugh. He has got away with a scratch.

For all its seriousness this crash has a comic side to it. The cause of it was the fact that the rudder-bar had been moved forward to accommodate the long legs of the previous pilot. In the hustle and bustle of our departure no one remembered to put it back. Kranz is quite a little fellow, and to make matters worse he was hampered by all the extra kit he was wearing. But he did not notice that his feet could not reach the rudder-bar until he was in the air, and then it was too late. We both could not help roaring with laughter, and I was happy to see him safe and sound. One good result from the crash, at any rate, is that we shall have another officer travelling with the Staffel.

I give orders for the two machines left behind to be burnt with the tents and other material; then I climb in again. The machines in the air are circling round the aerodrome above my head. My engine starts to run and I give the "all clear" signal. Once more my eyes wander over the aerodrome and its hangars; a number of men come rushing up and want to shake hands. Good bye, good bye, all of you!

My clock shows 11.30 a.m. I push my goggles down and open the throttle.

My last take off!

Once round the aerodrome—then the other machines collect around me and drop into their usual positions. I see the men below me waving their caps and handkerchiefs; then I put my machine into a southeasterly course.

One last look back shows me a tent in flames. A thick cloud of smoke rises up from it. Our home is being destroyed. There is no haven of refuge for us now—and no turning back is possible.

The flames increase, and the smoke mingles with the clouds.

I stare ahead of me, trying to steer a course by my compass. Unpleasant flying to-day, because the clouds prevent us from going higher than five hundred metres. The cloud eddies rock and pull our machines, while sidewinds push them out of the course. But there are eleven machines behind me, flying in Staffel formation. Helmo is close on one side of me, in Schmidt's place; we often nod to one another and discuss our route in the language of signs. As a matter of fact our flight is a very uncertain affair; at this low height we cannot get a general view of the country, and there were very few landmarks to guide us. Our only help lies in the compass, but even with its aid we cannot be certain of the drift.

The broad ribbon of the Meuse lies below us. The clouds are lifting somewhat, and so we can gain height. We have no notion where we are; the ground below is hilly and wooded. Villages loom into sight and disappear; we pass over roads and fly along railway lines.

On we go—southeastward.

The clouds continue to rise until we get a ceiling at one thousand metres, but below us the ground is covered with a huge milk-white cloth—fog. That is the worst that can befall us, but we have no choice; we must carry on as long as our petrol holds out. We can only hope that we may find an end to this fog-blanket somewhere.

We are swimming in a huge, grey box. Over our heads is the cloud ceiling, below us a sea of fog. Only at very rare intervals do we catch sight of a green patch or a white road through a hole in the fog. And so we continue to steer southeast by the compass.

12.30 p.m. According to my calculations we ought to be somewhere over Luxemburg. But the fog does not break; it only grows thicker.

Marx lays his machine beside mine and signals that he must make a forced landing. I see him go down and disappear in the mist, but cannot discover what happens to him below, because we others have to carry on.

Doubts rise up in my mind. Will my compass be reliable, or will it have been too much influenced by the clouds? Has the side-wind drifted us too far out of our course? The space between clouds and fog is nothing else than a vast coffin which holds us prisoned inside its gloomy walls.

At last I catch sight of a deep furrow in the sea of clouds. That must be the course of a river—of a large river. The Moselle? It is time we reached it, and there is no other large river on our route.

We drop to hover over a deep valley, from which the broad bends of a winding river gleam dully upward. That must certainly

be the Moselle, on which lies Metz. But I have no notion whereabouts we have hit the river. If we go up stream, we shall get into
France, but a down-stream course will certainly take us to Germany.

We therefore fly down stream. That is the safest plan, and we
are sure to come to a town some time; besides, there are many fog-
free areas by the river, so that we have a chance of making a good
landing somewhere. For the present, however, there does not seem
any likelihood of a landing place, because the banks fall steeply to
the river and there is no level ground anywhere.

Our flight continues. Gradually petrol gets low, thus adding to
our troubles. The Pfalz machines have smaller tanks than the
Fokkers and will run out of juice first. So we shall have to land
somewhere soon.

The fog is as thick as ever. No landing place, not a sign of a
field anywhere. In a few minutes we shall have to come down, and
then we are done for.

But now a small hole in the clouds gapes before me, revealing
a strip of meadowland. It is far from level ground; it is undulating,
with a slight slope, but good enough to try a forced landing. I see
a few huts at the edge of it and an anti-aircraft gun in position. Perhaps it is a parade ground.

We have no choice. There is thick fog all around us; our petrol
is nearly done. This is a chance that Fate offers us.

I give the signal to land and drop down. My Verey light shoots
down to the meadow in a wide sweep and burns and smokes to its
end on the grass. The smoke rises straight up; it therefore does not
matter from which direction we land.

My machine flattens out, touches the ground and then comes
to a standstill. I taxi on towards the hut to make room for the others and wait for them to land.

The place does not turn out to be anything like as good as it appeared from above. It contains a number of hollows, and three of my pilots come to grief in them. Their machines sustain light damage, but all the rest make good landings.

Where are we?

A couple of Landsturmers approach us and give the information. We are close to Trier.

Trier?—Trier! then we are well out of our course; the wind has drifted us a longish way to north.

"What's up here?" we ask.

"There's nothing here but an Archie battery. This is an old parade-ground."

"Have you got any petrol here, or can we find any in the neighbourhood?"

"No, there's none here. But there's an aircraft park in Trier."

"An aircraft park?" Then we are in luck's way; we can get all we want there. "But whereabouts is Trier?"

"Just down there." The Landsturm man indicates the direction with his pipe.

He is right; down there in the depths there lies a large town. And then we catch sight of a large, level meadow, with many sheds and huts—the aircraft park.

We could not see it from the air because it was covered by the fog. Now we are all mightily pleased because we had lost our belief in the existence of such facilities. Everyone of us had pictured the inevitable crash if he had tried to land anywhere down there. So we decide to fly there; it is barely a couple of minutes away.

But it is not advisable to let the damaged machines take off. We therefore push the three of them to the huts and put them in charge of the Archie battery's crew. Their pilots can make their way on foot to the aircraft park.

We others take off. It only needs a little gas to get us into the air; then we can glide the rest of the way. It is not long before we all make good landings on the aerodrome.

We taxi to the hangars there. But no one comes to meet us; not a soul takes any notice of our arrival.

I go into one of the sheds, accost a group of mechanics that are lounging about idly and ask them to direct me to the officer on duty.

"There are no officers here," is the answer. "There's a soldiers' council in charge now."

"To whom do I apply for petrol then?"

"There's no petrol to be had. The soldiers' council has stopped its issue."

No petrol? I talk the situation over with my pilots. We decide that we must do all we can to get some petrol, because we want to continue our flight tomorrow.

We tried our best, but we could not get any from the park—not even by back-stair methods. So I took the tram into the town to find the local commandant, but the people in his office knew of no way to help me; they had abdicated all their authority to the soldiers' council.

The soldiers' council declined to give me any assistance. They needed all the petrol for their cars, they said, and could not spare any for aircraft,—and least of all for officer pilots.

I went to the gasworks and other works in the hope of getting some—but all in vain. The impressions I gained in Trier were the worst possible; the town was a hotbed of mutiny and disorder. We were not prepared for anything of that sort, because we were accustomed to the good spirit shown by our own men and could not believe that all discipline would crumble away so quickly.

All the streets were full of riot and uproar, red flag processions and revolutionary oratory. The greater part of the demonstrants was composed of women and young lads.

I saw a mob assault an officer at a street corner. I went for

them at once, but my help came too late. I found the old officer
lying on the ground, with his head bleeding from several wounds.
His uniform was in tatters; the epaulettes that had been torn off
lay in the mud. I was in time to rescue him and carry him off to
safety in a neighbouring hotel.

I could not understand the hatred shown by those people.
What harm had the old officer done them? Was it their hatred of
the system under which the individual had to suffer?

And what if the mob should choose to fall upon me? Was that
our thanks for having kept the enemy out of the country for so
many years?

The afternoon was waning. I took a tram back to the park and
told my pilots of my failure.

So we cannot continue our flight.

But there is still some petrol left in every machine. We empty
the tanks and transfer the liquid into two machines which will thus
be able to take off tomorrow and fly to Bavaria. We others will
have to continue our journey by train.

We render the other machines unserviceable. I cut a large strip
out of the side of my cockpit and pick it up. Then I remove the
handle of my stick, with the trigger button attached to it and take
it with me as a souvenir. For a long while we stand beside our machines; it is so inexpressibly hard to part from them.

At last we march off to the tram halt.

The mechanics have given us a good natured warning to remove our epaulettes and cockades, because the mob in the town
are hunting down all the officers they find. But we refuse to follow
their advice; we shall just leave it to chance whether anyone spots
us; if so, we shall know how to defend ourselves. We have lost so
much that it does not seem to matter to us whether we lose our
lives as well. But as we are carrying our luggage we do not look
particularly like officers, and in any case the thick fur collars of our

overcoats conceal the epaulettes. Moreover it has grown dark since our arrival at Trier.

We find quarters in a hotel near the station and get an evening meal. Tomorrow we shall continue our journey by the earliest possible train. There is no good in trying to do anything in this place; the best thing is to go to bed.

12.11.18. 4.30 a.m.: train to Saarbrücken. We were lucky to catch it; it was the last train that went off in accordance with the timetable.

Hess and Stoer took off early in the morning. Hess had a forced landing at Mannheim, where he crashed his machine, but Stoer flew across the Palatinate to Bavaria and landed at the depot in Furth. His was the only machine belonging to the Staffel that reached its destination.

We others reached Saarbrücken at 8 a.m. There we were joined by two officers from Staffel 34 who had written off their machines in a forced landing in the neighbourhood.

11.30 a.m.: departure from Saarbrücken, During the journey we discussed all possibilities. We felt that everything had changed, but we knew nothing that was certain, and the new order of things was so alien to us that we could not adapt ourselves to it. The defence of the frontier seemed to be the task nearest to our hands.

We could not understand what was happening in our country, because we did not realise how far the disintegration had gone. Therefore we thought the most important thing was to defend the land against the foe without, to guard its frontiers.

We wanted to fly and fight to the end.

13.11.18. 1.30 a.m.: arrival at Munich. It was with very strange feelings that we saw the train glide into the vast station, for that was not at all the sort of homecoming we had imagined.

Heavily armed sailors and other fellows in uniform stood at the barrier; they wanted to search us for concealed weapons and called on us to remove our fur coats. We did not vouchsafe them a word, but our threatening looks sufficed to make them open up a passage for us at once. No one else had any desire to try to obtain our arms or coats.

How we despised and loathed those fellows!

We parted outside the station. A last handshake; then each went his own way.

Helmo and I went together for a long stretch. The streets were dead; the squares gaped like huge, burnt-out craters. Our footsteps echoed on the nightly pavements, beating an eerie accompaniment to the music of loneliness.

We strode through an alien, empty town. It was the end.

The next few days passed like a dream, like the delirium begotten of fever. I met many old friends, I reported myself at the headquarters of our air force and was given temporary leave.

21.11.18. The men of the Staffel arrived at Schleissheim. They were discharged or sent on leave; I saw only a few of them again. Wart was blissfully happy at meeting his master once more.

25.11.18. The lorries arrived with our baggage. The drivers had great difficulty in getting them through and protecting them from the soldiers' councils that wanted to take forcible possession of them. But their contents remained intact; not a single piece of baggage was missing; even the gramophone records lay just where we had put them.

Events are taking their course. The war is over. No Staffels have been called up for frontier defence.

The land lies open and unprotected. It seethes and rages within. I drift on the surface, as on a dim, gloomy sea, and can play no further part in what takes place.

Once again several weeks have rolled by. A courier Staffel has been instituted for express postal communication between Munich and Nürnberg. Greim and I have been taken on as old war pilots.

So once again I am sitting in a machine; I have an aerodrome and an objective When I take off from Nürnberg, with the Danube gleaming beneath me, the whole horizon ahead reveals a long, jagged chain of shining peaks, a line of petrified waves—the Alps. Wherever my eye wanders, it beholds the beauty of a peaceful land.

These are the glorious flights in the homeland, to which we looked forward with such delight.

The fair countryside rolls past below me. But my eyes are not yet accustomed to looking for beauty on the ground below; my senses still judge everything by war standards. For me yonder wooded patch might harbour an Archie battery, while the village over there could contain a munition dump. By force of habit I search the sky around me; my eyes are looking out for enemy aircraft.

But no shell-burst rises up, no machine swoops out of the sun. An infinite desolation grips at my heart. The engine roars its wonted, monotonous song, the valves before me move in an infinitely even rhythm.

I start as though suddenly roused from sleep and search the air—no machine—nothing.

Loneliness—unending loneliness.

These are the glorious flights in the homeland, to which we looked forward with such delight!

Home has become a strange land to us. We cannot find our way back. We have lost our home.

The land that encircles us is an alien land. The life that swallows us up is an alien life.

We live in a strange country that we cannot know. Our home— our home is dead.

And this home of ours was the Staffel.